JOSHUA

SLAVE, UNDERSTUDY, WARRIOR, SPY, SUCCESSOR, CONQUEROR, AND RULER

LOUIS MCCALL

Joshua

Slave, Understudy, Warrior, Spy, Successor, Conqueror, and Ruler

By

Louis McCall

FOREWORD

Joshua: Slave, Understudy, Warrior, Spy, Successor, Conqueror and Ruler
Pastor Joel Schmidgall
National Community Church

Dr. McCall is one of the unique authors that can take historical facts, Biblical account, and good storytelling and weave them together to produce an insightful and interesting journey through the most famous ancient text. He doesn't just write from book knowledge, but from personal exploration through the geography of the text.

In this book, he takes on one of the most courageous characters in the scriptures. If you like an underdog story, you'll love Joshua. A man who started in the lowest of positions and ascended to the highest, while leading a small nation of former slaves to the long-awaited promise land. Receive Dr. McCall's reminder to not underestimate what God wants to do in and through you, as you read this bold declaration of all things becoming possible.

DEDICATION

I dedicate this book to God the Holy Spirit. It was He that moved me to delve into the story of Joshua and write this book. He also drew me to Egypt and Jordan in January 2024, where I gained an appreciation of the context and the landscape. He also arranged for me to spend valuable time with an Egyptology academic expert who introduced me to the history of Hatshepsut, the female Pharaoh, and her mortuary temple, which I visited. This spurred me to dig into archives and the research of others that enabled me to place her story in the story of Moses and see something I had never seen before about the man who became the mentor and collaborator to Joshua, finally ordaining Joshua to take his place at God's direction.

As I considered writing this book, I looked for confirmation. One confirmation was my chance encounter with a young man named Josh while traveling through the countryside of the state of Maryland. I told Josh, I am an author of Christian books and you are my confirmation today. He seemed stunned and wanted to know what I meant by that. Then I explained that I was praying about writing a book about Joshua, and he, Josh, was my confirmation that day to proceed. Josh then stuck with me for quite a while, intrigued by how he was being used in this endeavor and telling me about his life. The Holy Spirit brought us together and enlightened the day for me and Josh.

ACKNOWLEDGMENTS

The King James Version of the Holy Bible served as the sourcebook for this fictional account. Although fictional, this book is based on what is recorded in the Bible. Where dialogue is taken from the Bible, it was paraphrased by the author into modern colloquial English. Other dialogue comes from the artistic license of the author and is fictional.

Scripture quotations are from The Authorized (King James) Version. Rights in the Authorized Version in the United Kingdom are vested in the Crown and are reproduced by permission of the Crown's patentee, Cambridge University Press. I also want to acknowledge my dear wife Lenora's helpful assistance and patience. Her sharp eyes and constructive criticism contributed significantly to improving this book.

ENDORSEMENTS

Louis McCall's **Joshua** brings to life the beautiful biblical account of the beginning of God's kingdom people, the Israelites. McCall's use of conversation and descriptive detail makes the reader feel like a part of the narrative as the real and imagined characters converse and walk through history. For a non-Christian or a new believer, it is a revelation of God's hand in man's affairs. It may well be the testimony that someone needs to hear to realize who Jesus was. The accuracy of biblical and historical events accentuates the relevancy of the book for today.

Sara Lewis

Author of *Purposeful People-Pleasing: Changing Your Perspective Not Your Personality* and *Called to Pray: An Intercessor's Toolkit.*

Hostess of National Community Church's Writer's Courtyard.

In **Joshua: Slave, Understudy, Warrior, Spy, Successor, Conqueror, and Ruler**, Louis McCall offers a masterful exploration of one of history's most fascinating figures. McCall's witty and engaging dialogue brings the story to life, transforming complex historical and theological concepts into an accessible and captivating narrative.

The author's extensive knowledge of the Hebrew people's history and theology is evident throughout the book. McCall's insights into Joshua's multifaceted roles are

informative and deeply enriching, providing a nuanced understanding of the historical and spiritual significance of this key biblical figure.

The book is easy to read. McCall expertly balances scholarly depth with a compelling storytelling style that is enjoyable for casual readers and those with a deeper background.

Joshua is a remarkable contribution to biblical studies. It blends intellectual rigor with engaging and creative prose. It is an essential read for anyone interested in the rich tapestry of biblical history and the enduring legacy of its characters.

Kelvin K. Mulembe, DMin, MDiv
Pastor, Arlington Temple United
Methodist Church
Arlington, Virginia

In this historical fiction account of the life of Joshua, author Louis McCall weaves together a beautiful tapestry of a courageous military man who loved God and longed to rest in His presence.

The biblical account of Joshua's pilgrimage is interfaced with factual and geographical data from that time, offering a third dimension to this story.

Joshua became a wise man after a lifetime of walking with the Lord through many unconventional military battles as well as filling Moses' shoes to lead God's people into the Promised Land. A path not designed for the faint of heart, Joshua rose to the challenge.

Legacy is an important theme in this book, as God's truth and miraculous power are passed along from generation to generation. May we not take for granted the miracles God blesses us with daily.

McCall's book **"Joshua"** passes along this commission to us, telling the story of God's faithfulness to all people. It is through our obedience, as we trust Him, that He can do mighty things among us for His honor and glory.

Barbara Hollace, JD
Author of multiple books including the
Miracle Man Trilogy
Communications Director, Spokane Dream Center, Spokane Valley, WA
Global Prayer Ministry Pastor

The author of **Joshua** has written this book in a very unique and beautiful way. The author describes Joshua telling the whole story of how God fulfilled his promise to Abraham. And told how 70 people went to Egypt and stayed there for 400 years. There, the challenges and problems faced by the Israelites are described in detail, including how Moses was born with the mission to lead the Israelites from Egypt to the Promised Land. Each episode is uniquely and beautifully told. I learned a lot and was blessed by reading this wonderful book. I think everyone should read this book and be blessed!

Bishop Qamar Aziz
Independent Evangelistic Outreach Ministries
Punjab, Pakistan

Louis McCall has done it yet again! With an unwavering commitment to sharing the stories of our leaders and the

people of God, he brings us the tale of **Joshua**, a man who began as a slave but rose to become a triumphant figure of faith. Through Louis' writing, we are reminded that God is bigger than any obstacle we may face and that with determination and faith, we can overcome anything. A truly uplifting read that will leave you feeling inspired and empowered!

"As for me and my house, we will serve the Lord."

Pastor L. S. Greene
The New Beginning Church
Lipscomb, AL 35020

It is with warm endearment that I recommend **Joshua: Slave, Understudy, Warrior, Spy, Successor, Conqueror and Ruler** to every reader's library of Bible book stories. This phenomenal book is filled with historical elements, hidden mysteries, and confirmed artifacts from Joshua's life. The profound author, Louis McCall, has mastered the details surrounding the life of Joshua, the "Great Deliverer." As you read, you will relate to and enjoy the time period of the Pharaohs and how Joshua's life was used by God.

I would recommend this book to all Christians who are seeking to learn more about Joshua's life and how their lives can be a mirror of great success and leave a legacy for generations to come as a likeness to **Joshua: Slave, Understudy, Warrior, Spy, Successor, Conqueror, and Ruler**.

Dr. JaVon Ophelia Butler, MPA
Founder, Writer, Director, and Producer
Selah Productions, Inc.

TABLE OF CONTENTS

CHAPTER 1

Joshua Faces Retirement and Awaits His End

Joshua's Adventure is Nearly Complete

The 108-year-old Joshua walked into his comfortable house from his courtyard and sat down. Still a powerful-looking former warrior, he looked heavenward and mused aloud to himself, "I've come a long way from spending over 40 years in tents in the desert!" Joshua called for his attendant, the grandson of Oholiab, who God anointed to assist Bezalel with the artisan work on the Tabernacle and the golden Ark of the Covenant. When the attendant, who was also called Oholiab, entered, Joshua kindly asked him to untie and set aside his sandals. After taking a drink of water from a cup and pitcher brought in by Oholiab, Joshua took a few deep breaths. He began to utter praises to God for His goodness, only to be interrupted by a clamor outside.

The security guard was contending with a small band of children, girls, and boys between ten and fourteen years of age. Joshua asked Oholiab to find out what the ruckus was all about. Oholiab returned to report, "There is a group of children outside, and they want to see

you, but the guard intended to gruffly send them away back to their mothers."

When Joshua heard Oholiab's report, he said, "Let the children come to me. Am I not a father in Israel? Some call me the father of the nation. If so, then I am also a father to them." With that, Oholiab fetched the children and brought them to Joshua, who asked, "Why do you want to see me? I have already divided up the land of Canaan and those lands on the other side of the Jordan River that we took possession of when King Sihon of the Amorites and King Og of Bashan, who was a giant, withstood us, rather than allow us to pass through their lands for a fee and were utterly defeated. What is your request?"

"My name is Ephraim" said the older boy, "and my friend is Jacob." "And my name is Miriam," said the older girl, "and Sarah is with me." Ephraim continued, "We want you to tell us the story of our people. We heard that you are the oldest living person in our nation, and there is nothing you don't know."

Joshua began, "Our story is summed up in this: trust God, obey His commandments, seek Him with a pure heart, be courageous and not fearful, and He will deliver. Only serve Him and Him alone because He is the only God. All other gods are idols crafted by the hands of man from wood, clay, stone, or metal.

Moreover, He has chosen us to be His people."

"Lord Joshua," pleaded Ephraim, "Please tell us the whole story in detail, and we will patiently hear you out."

Joshua Recounts the History of the People and His Own Role in it

Joshua laughed, saying, "I am not so old that I was a witness to the entire story of our people, but I will do my best. For the Hebrew people, it began when Yahweh called Abraham out of Ur of the Chaldeans in Mesopotamia when he was 75 years old and told him to leave his people, who were idol worshippers, and go to a land He would show him. God brought Abraham to Canaan and told him the land would be his and his descendants. Abraham and his wife Sarah were both old and childless. Yet in time, when Abraham was 100 and his wife Sarah was 90, God gave Abraham a son by Sarah. That promised child was named Isaac. Being warned by God that Isaac should not take a wife of the Canaanites, Abraham sent his servant to find a wife for Isaac from his kindred in Mesopotamia. When Yahweh commanded Abraham to take his promised son and sacrifice him, Abraham obeyed. Since Yahweh had promised Abraham that he would be the father of many nations, Abraham believed that Yahweh would have to raise Isaac from the dead to keep his promise if he, Abraham, followed

through and sacrificed his son. When Yahweh saw that Abraham was willing to sacrifice his son, He, through His angel, forbade Abraham not to harm the lad and directed him to a ram caught in a thicket to offer instead. For his part, Isaac also acted in faith and did not resist or fight his father, knowing the promises of God that Abraham had shared with him.

"During their lives, both Abraham and Isaac lived in the land of the Philistines and prospered there until, in each case, they were asked to leave. Nevertheless, each made a covenant with the Philistine king they called Abimelech, at the initiative of the Philistine king and the captain of the Philistine army. Abraham dwelt in that land for 26 years. (Genesis 21:22-27) Isaac dwelt in Gerar of the Philistines after Yahweh told him not to go to Egypt. He had problems with the son of Abimelech because Yahweh prospered him so much that the Philistines envied him. (Genesis 26:1-31) Isaac and his wife Rebecca had twin sons, Esau and Jacob. Esau took two Hittite women as wives, which vexed Isaac and Rebecca. (Genesis 26:34) Because Jacob, whose name means deceiver, cunningly stole Esau's birthright and Isaac's blessing to the firstborn, Jacob fled for his life to his relatives in Mesopotamia. There, he worked for his uncle Laban and married two of Laban's daughters, Leah and Rachel. In time, Jacob had 12 sons from Leah, Rachel, and their handmaids, whom they gave to Jacob, counting the offspring

as their own. In leaving Laban and returning to the land of Canaan, Yahweh appeared to Jacob just as He had appeared to Abraham. Jacob made peace with his brother Esau and dwelt in Canaan.

"For spite, Jacob's favorite son by Rachel, named Joseph, was sold into slavery and taken to Egypt by Midianite traders who resold Joseph to a high-ranking Egyptian. In the meantime, Joseph's brothers convinced their father that wild beasts had torn Joseph to pieces and presented their father with the torn and blood-soaked coat worn by Joseph. Over 14 years, Joseph served his Egyptian master Potiphar and then was imprisoned when Potiphar's wife accused Joseph of attempted rape when in fact, he fled from her attempt to seduce him. But Yahweh raised Joseph from prison, and by giving him the interpretation of the Egyptian Pharaoh's troubling dreams, Pharaoh elevated Joseph to second in the land only to Pharaoh to prepare for the famine Joseph foretold.

God's Prophesy to Abraham Begins to Unfold

"When the famine came, it afflicted Jacob and his sons, their wives, and children in Canaan, too. In the process of sending his sons to Egypt to buy grain, it was eventually revealed that Joseph was the powerful man they bowed down to. Joseph had great favor with Pharaoh and was allowed to fetch Jacob and all his people, 70 in all, to come and live in Goshen in lower

Egypt. Now Yahweh had revealed to Abraham that His people, Israel, would be enslaved in a strange land for 400 years until the sin of the Canaanites was full, and then they would return to and possess the land promised to Abraham. In addition, Yahweh promised Abraham that he would judge the nation that would enslave and oppress his descendants." (Genesis 15:13-16)

CHAPTER 2

Remembering Slavery and Oppression in Egypt

Going from Honor and Respect to Becoming Despised Slaves

"Because of Joseph, we Hebrews were treated as honored guests in Egypt. However, in time, a Pharaoh who did not know Joseph arose. (Exodus 1:8-11) That Pharaoh and his people were foreigners who had migrated from the east to the kingdom of lower Egypt. As foreigners, they were called Hyksos.[1] They eventually fought and overcame the original Egyptians but ruled as Egyptians in the style of the Pharaohs over lower Egypt, while native Egyptians continued to rule upper Egypt to the south. Thus, the goodwill that came down to the Hebrews in Goshen because of the high esteem in which Joseph was held was forgotten. Therefore, we became slaves to the Hyksos for two centuries until they were overthrown by the native Egyptians and forced back to the lands to the east in Canaan. However, our numbers multiplied such that the Egyptians feared us. Their solution was to keep us enslaved, as we had been under the Hyksos, and oppress us. One Pharaoh even hatched a plan to kill newborn male Hebrews at birth.

"The Egypt I, Joshua, grew up in was a place of enslavement and oppression by cruel taskmasters. My name was Hoshea of the tribe of Ephraim, and my father, Nun, was a prince of the tribe of Ephraim. I was and am a direct descendant of Joseph. Nevertheless, my life was a life of drudgery and the repeated sting of the Egyptian taskmaster's lash.

"I, Joshua, spent my days making bricks from mud and straw. I would haul mud up from the Nile River delta, which included the area of Goshen where we Hebrews lived. The mud was put into large pits and chopped straw was added to the pits. Initially, the Egyptians supplied the straw. I and other young men marched around the pits using our feet to mix the straw with the mud. My leg muscles grew quite strong. While I marched in the pits mixing chopped straw with the mud, the women and old men scooped up the mixture, put it into molds, and then released the form from the molds to dry in the sun. Once sun-dried, the bricks were put into kilns and treated with fire to strengthen them. The bricks we made were used by the Egyptians to build structures in Pharaoh's storage cities at Pithom and Rameses. (Exodus 1:11)

"We had to grow our own food, which involved catching fish and growing leeks, onions, garlic, and grain for breadmaking, as well as raising other items. We would also trade with those who brought foodstuffs down the Nile River

in their boats. We also tended cattle for the Egyptians and had cattle of our own from the sheep we had introduced from Canaan. The Egyptians did not like the idea of herding sheep and were happy to leave that to us.

"Although we were Hebrews, being in Egypt and in bondage for generations took a toll on our faith. Many forgot the covenant our ancestors made with Yahweh. Because the Egyptians worshipped many gods, and they were over us, many Hebrews gradually came to worship the gods of Egypt, along with Yahweh, or to worship the gods of Egypt alone. We had no principal place of worship and we had no priests of Yahweh. We were enslaved, but we were becoming like the very Egyptians whom we despised.

Moses Born With A Mission

"As the Egyptians increased their oppression, we sighed and grew increasingly depressed over the situation. Thus, we cried out to Yahweh for deliverance. I, Joshua, learned of a Hebrew named Moses who had been raised in the house of Pharaoh as a prince of Egypt and the adopted son of the daughter of Pharaoh Thutmosis I.[2] That Pharaoh's daughter was Hatshepsut. She was but a child when she adopted Moses and gave him a name like that of her father. She asked a Hebrew girl named Mariam to find a Hebrew woman to nurse Moses,

not knowing Mariam was the sister of Moses and the woman who nursed Moses was his actual mother. Thus, Moses stayed with his real mother until he was weaned at about age four or five. After that, he was taken into the Pharoah's household, raised, and educated there. Pharoah Thutmosis I had no sons by his primary wife. He eventually sired a son, Thutmosis II, from a secondary wife and died shortly afterward. When Tutmosis I died, Hatshepsut ruled as regent because her half-brother Thutmosis II was a minor. She eventually ruled as a Pharoah and dressed as a Pharoah to the point of wearing a pasted-on beard, even when Thutmosis II came of age. Thutmosis II then married his half-sister Hatshepsut to legitimize himself further since Hatshepsut was born of the queen. Hatshepsut bore no male heirs to Thutmosis II, but he did get a son named Thutmosis III by a secondary wife. All the while, Moses grew up in the royal household. After Thutmosis II died, Hatshepsut again ruled as co-regent, this time with her stepson Thutmosis III. There eventually arose a strife between Thutmosis III and Moses after the death of Hatshepsut. When Moses unsuccessfully attempted to lead a slave uprising and killed an Egyptian who was abusing a Hebrew, he fled to Midian for 40 years while Pharoah Thutmosis III ruled. (Exodus 2:11-15) I, Joshua, was born when Moses went into exile at the age of 40. For our part, we endured and survived. We were hopeless, yet we cried out to Yahweh, hoping against hope

for deliverance. Miraculously, Yahweh heard our cry, which came up to His ears. He had pity on us and determined to send a deliverer."

Statue of the female Pharoah Hatshepsut, who adopted Moses and her shown as the male god Osiris in Luxor, formerly Thebes. ID 80975730 © Mareandmare Dreamstime.com

Large Kneeling Statue of Hatshepsut. Credit The Rogers Fund, 1930.

Available under The Met's Open Access Policy as being in the Public Domain.

The mortuary Temple of Hatshepsut. ID 187529011 © Alfredo Garcia Saz Dreamstime.com

CHAPTER 3

Change Came
God Appoints Moses as Deliverer of His Hebrew People

"One day, the 80-year-old Moses came to us out of Midian together with his wife, the daughter of the priest of Midian, his children, and his older brother Aaron, who had temporarily left Goshen to seek Moses. Yahweh had consented to let Aaron be Moses' mouthpiece. Also, Aaron confirmed the news that Yahweh revealed to Moses that Pharoah Thutmosis III and the men of his court who sought his life were dead. (Exodus 4:10-19) When Moses returned to Egypt, Pharaoh Amenhotep II, the surviving son of Thutmosis III, ruled and was also the step-nephew to Moses.

Ephraim asked, "Just how did Yahweh speak to Moses about these things?"

Joshua explained, "Moses was attracted, out of curiosity, one day, by a bush that burned but was not consumed. As he drew closer, Yahweh's voice called out to him from the burning bush and instructed him to take off his shoes because the ground he was on was holy. Then Yahweh revealed the assignment He was giving Moses. At first, Moses tried to beg out of the mission and wanted to excuse himself because he was given to stutter. Yahweh even became angry

with Moses because he was slow to obey and provided his brother Aaron as a mouthpiece for him. Moses and Aaron then went to Egypt.

"Moses and Aaron called together the elders of the Israelite tribes. (Exodus 4:29) Moses then rehearsed all of the things that Yahweh told him to do and speak. To confirm that Yahweh had sent him, Moses demonstrated signs that Yahweh had given him. Moses had Aaron take the staff of God from him and throw it on the ground, whereupon it became a snake. The elders all stepped back in fear until Moses instructed Aaron to take the snake by its tail, causing it to return to the form of the staff and give it back to him. The next sign was seen when Moses put his hand in the bosom of his robe. When he pulled it out again, it was leprous. As Moses held his hand up for all to see and walked around, the elders fled in panic, fearing they would be stricken with leprosy. When Moses put his hand in his bosom a second time, it was restored when he pulled it back out.

"After witnessing the signs, the tribal elders believed Yahweh had sent Moses. They were overjoyed to hear that Yahweh had seen their miserable situation and was concerned for their welfare. At that point, the elders bowed down and worshipped Yahweh. (Exodus 4:30-31)

"My father Nun was one of the elders for the tribe of Ephraim and was present at the introduction of Moses and Aaron. He relayed to me, Joshua, the skepticism of the elders until Moses and Aaron performed the signs given to them by Yahweh. Everyone was excited in anticipation of what was about to happen.

"After the meeting with the tribal elders, Moses, still known in Egypt, and Aaron called on the Pharaoh and said 'Yahweh,' that is the LORD, 'says Let My people go!'

God Makes Moses Like a God to Pharaoh

"Pharaoh, being prideful and believing that he himself was a god, said, 'Who is the LORD, that I should obey Him and let Israel go? I don't know the LORD, and I will not let Israel go.' Pharaoh also rebuked Moses and Aaron, commanding the people to return to work.

"That same day, Pharaoh ordered the slave drivers to no longer provide straw for brickmaking but have the slaves gather straw themselves without a reduction in their daily quota. Speaking of the Hebrews, Pharaoh said, 'They are lazy! Make their work so hard that they will not listen to the lies of Moses and Aaron.'

"The slave drivers kept pressing the slaves to meet the daily quota of bricks and beat the Hebrew foremen they had appointed when the

quota was not met. The Hebrew foremen went to the Pharaoh and complained that it was the fault of the Egyptians that the quota for bricks was not met because there was no straw. But the Pharaoh scolded them, calling them 'lazy' and commanding them to get back to work and maintain the tally of bricks without straw being provided.

"The foremen returned, and when they found Moses and Aaron waiting for them, they vented their anger, saying 'May the LORD judge you! You have made us to be a stench to Pharaoh and the slave drivers and have put a sword in their hands to kill us.' (Exodus 5:1-22)

"Moses turned to the LORD and complained about the trouble that had been stirred up and said, 'Is this why You sent me here? I went to Pharaoh in Your name, but he brought trouble on the people while You haven't rescued your people.'

The Beginning of God's Miraculous Wonders to Deliver His People

"The LORD then told Moses, 'Now you will see what I will do to Pharaoh. Because of my mighty hand, he won't just let them go; he will drive them out of his land.' The LORD added, 'I am the LORD. When I appeared to Abraham, Isaac, and Jacob, they knew me as God Almighty, but I was not known to them as Yahweh. I made

a covenant with them to give them the land of Canaan, where they were alien immigrants. I have heard the groans of the descendants of Israel. I am the LORD, and I will bring them out from under the burdens of the Egyptians, rid them of slavery, and redeem them with My stretched-out arm and great judgments. I will take them to Myself as a people, and I will be God to them, and they will know that I am the LORD their God that brought them out from under the burdens of the Egyptians. I will bring them into the land I promised to Abraham, Isaac, and Jacob and give it to them as their inheritance. I am the LORD.'

"Moses went back to the people and told them all of the things that the LORD had said, but they wouldn't listen to him because their spirits were downcast due to the increased oppression from the Egyptians.

Mariam asked, "Why were the Egyptians being so mean?"

Joshua replied, "It was of Yahweh that the heart of the Pharaoh became so stubborn so that the power of our God Yahweh could be demonstrated to be superior to Pharoah and the gods of Egypt. Yahweh told Moses to return to Pharaoh and command him to let the people go. But Moses told Yahweh that the Hebrews wouldn't even listen to him; how would Pharaoh pay heed to him? Besides, he said, 'I don't speak well.'

"Yahweh responded to Moses, 'I am making you a god to Pharaoh, and your brother Aaron shall be your prophet spokesperson. Just say what I command you, and your brother Aaron will speak it to Pharaoh. But I will harden the heart of Pharaoh against you so that I might multiply My signs and wonders in Egypt until the Egyptians know that I am the LORD and I bring out the descendants of Israel from among them.'"

CHAPTER 4

God's Power Demonstrated Over Pharaoh and the Gods of Egypt

Battle of the Gods

"Moses and Aaron returned to Pharaoh as the Lord instructed them. When Pharaoh Amenhotep II,[3] the step-grandson of Hatshepsut, demanded a sign of their authority, Moses gave his staff to Aaron and told him to throw it down. When Aaron threw down Moses's staff, it changed into a snake. It caused a stir in the palace around Pharaoh as Pharaoh's officers moved back out of the way.

"But Pharaoh beckoned to his head magicians Jannes and Jambres, who were experts in the dark knowledge of the Egyptians. Each magician, empowered by unseen evil angels, mumbled spells and threw down their staffs, which also became snakes. However, the smug looks on their faces soon melted away when Aaron's snake swallowed all of their snakes before Aaron took his snake by the tail, and it became a staff again. Pharaoh, however, was not impressed and still refused to let the people go.

"After Moses and Aaron left the audience with Pharaoh, God told Moses, 'Go tomorrow morning to Pharaoh while he is out in the river's water. Strike the river water with your staff, and it, together with the streams and ponds, will be turned to blood.'

"The next morning, Moses and Aaron did as Yahweh had instructed and encountered Pharaoh out in the water down from the steps of his palace. On either side of the steps leading into the water were giant images of Egyptian gods of the Nile. With his priests nearby, Pharaoh praised the Egyptian gods and goddess of the Nile, Apis and the goddess Isis along with Osiris. The Egyptians believed the Nile was the blood flowing in the veins of Osiris. In the sight of Pharaoh, Aaron took Moses' staff and struck the water, which then turned to blood.

"Pharaoh, his family, priests, and attendants all scurried out of the Nile and up the stairs, all bloodied. Their white linen tunics and skirts were all bloody on their lower portions. Not to be outdone, Pharaoh's magicians took containers of water and turned them into blood. Pharaoh remained steadfast in refusing to let the Hebrews go[4]. So, there was no water in Egypt to drink for seven days. Unable to breathe, the fish in the Nile died, floated to the surface, and washed up on the banks, creating a horrible stench. God, through Moses, had demonstrated His superiority over the gods of Egypt's Nile River.

However, there was plenty of fresh water in Goshen, where the Hebrews lived. Therefore, the Hebrews all began to respect Moses as he related his instructions from Yahweh and how he and Aaron demonstrated Yahweh's heavy hand on the Egyptians for refusing to let us go. I, Joshua, certainly was in awe of the godlike power demonstrated by Moses.

"Then God told Moses, 'Go back to Pharaoh and tell him the Lord says to let My people go so they may worship Me. If you refuse, I will send a plague of frogs throughout the entire country.'

"Moses did as God instructed. He and Aaron confronted Pharaoh with the words that God had commanded. When Pharaoh laughed and refused to let the people go, Moses handed his staff to Aaron and told him to stretch it out over the Nile's waters, tributary streams, and ponds and command frogs to come forth. Suddenly, an army of frogs came leaping out of the Nile. In the meantime, Moses and Aaron departed and returned to us in Goshen to leave the Egyptians with the plague of frogs.

Mariam interjected, "Frogs! I hate those nasty things. I would have given Moses what he wanted to avoid that plague!"

Joshua went on, "Frogs were everywhere, and the royal palace was no exception. The frogs got into everything. They were in the bedrooms and beds so that the Egyptians couldn't sleep.

Frogs got into the kitchens and the dough being made into bread. There was no place that was without the plague of frogs, except in Goshen where we Hebrews lived, because Yahweh did not visit the plagues on us.

"Frogs held a special place among the Egyptians. They were treated as sacred, and one was not supposed to kill them. They were a reminder of the goddess Heket, who was represented with a frog-like head and bulging eyes. To the Egyptians, Heket was the goddess of fertility and birth. Pharaoh's magicians showed him that they, too, could call up frogs from the Nile by calling on the goddess Heket, but more frogs were not the thing that was needed.

"Finally, Pharaoh sent for Moses and Aaron. When they arrived, Pharaoh said to Moses, 'Pray to the Lord to take away the frogs, and I will let your people go to sacrifice to the Lord.'

"Moses agreed and said, 'I will leave to you the honor of setting the time for me to pray so that you will be rid of the frogs, except for those that remain in the Nile.'

"For some inexplicable reason, Pharaoh said, 'Tomorrow!' rather than, 'Immediately!' When Moses did pray, the frogs died everywhere outside of the Nile. The dead frogs were everywhere: in homes, streets, and fields. They were swept out, shoveled up, carted away, and dumped into huge, stinking mounds.

"Once Pharaoh saw that the menace of the frogs was past, he reneged on his word and refused to let the Hebrews go and would not listen to Moses and Aaron. So, God told Moses, 'Tell Aaron to stretch out your staff and strike the ground. The dust will become gnats throughout the land.' Moses did so.

"With Pharaoh and his magicians watching, Aaron stretched out the staff of Moses and struck the ground. Immediately, the dust of the ground became alive with gnats that rose up and afflicted people and animals. Animals were bucking, biting, rolling in the dirt for relief, running into the Nile, and thrashing around. People were waving, scratching, and swatting. They covered their mouths and nostrils to keep the gnats out. They squinted and rubbed their eyes to keep the gnats from sucking up the moisture of their eyes. Once again, preparing meals without the gnats being in the food was impossible.

"When the magicians Jannes and Jambres tried to duplicate calling up gnats from the dust, they could not. They called on Set, the Egyptian god of the desert, represented by gnats. But it was to no avail. Turning to Pharaoh, they said, 'This is the finger of God!'

"Then the Lord spoke to Moses saying, 'Get up early in the morning and go confront Pharaoh

when he is in the water of the Nile. Tell him the Lord says let My people go so they may worship me, but if you do not let My people go, I will send swarms of flies. So that you will know that I am God, I will make a distinction between your people and My people in the land of Goshen. This sign will occur tomorrow. While you have flies, there will be no flies in Goshen, where My people live.'

"Moses did as instructed, and a plague of flies came over Egypt. The Egyptian god Uatchit was the fly god, but no one was happy with the plague of flies. They were in everything. The flies fouled the food for meals and would bite. Children cried, herds of animals stampeded, and people swatted and beat themselves with whatever would temporarily cause the flies to get off them.

"Finally, once again, Pharaoh summoned Moses and Aaron. He said, 'Go ahead and sacrifice to your God, but do not go far. Stay nearby.'

"Moses responded, 'That will not work. We have to go on a three-day journey into the wilderness. Besides, you Egyptians find our sacrifices to be detestable to you.' So, the Pharaoh agreed to Moses's stipulation. Turning to leave, Moses said, 'I will pray to the Lord to remove the flies tomorrow, but you must not go back on your word this time and refuse to let the people go.'

"However, once the flies were gone, Pharaoh ordered the overlords and army not to let the Hebrews go.

"Yahweh again sent Moses and Aaron to confront Pharaoh. He told Moses, 'Tell Pharaoh that the God of the Hebrews says let My people go, so that they may worship me. But if you refuse to let them go, I will send a plague on all of your livestock in the country so that they all die. However, I will make a distinction for My people in Goshen. Not one of the animals that they own will die.'

"Again, Moses did as instructed, but Pharaoh refused to relent and let the people go. As the animals of Egypt were stricken, Pharaoh had his priests and magicians appeal to the god Apis and the goddess Hathor, the images of both of whom were of cattle. But it was to no avail. So, all of Egypt's cattle, camels, sheep, and goats died. Pharaoh sent people to observe the situation in Goshen, and they reported that none of the cattle belonging to the Hebrews had died. In the meantime, the Egyptians had to bury all of the dead cattle. Consequently, no milk was available for drinking, cheese making, or other dairy products. Neither was there fresh meat to eat, draft oxen to plow fields, or pull carts. Even so, Pharaoh refused to let the Hebrews go.

"Then Yahweh instructed Moses to go before Pharaoh to pronounce a plague of boils. Standing before Pharaoh, Moses took some ashes

that he had brought, as instructed by God, and tossed them into the air. The ashes spread through Egypt and became painful boils. The magicians of Pharaoh were so stricken that they ran from Moses shrieking in pain. Even as Pharaoh and his family and officials struggled with the painful boils, Pharaoh continued to refuse to let us Hebrews go.

"Later, Yahweh told Moses to get up in the morning and go to confront Pharaoh again. This time, the message was that there would be a plague of hail and fire if the Hebrews were not allowed to leave. Moses did as he was instructed. He warned the Pharaoh that anyone who did not seek shelter would be killed by the plague. So, the Pharaoh was given time to put out the word so that people could get into their homes. However, Pharaoh and his priests prayed to Set the storm god and to Nut, the sky goddess, to block the threat coming from Moses and the God of the Hebrews. It was a vain attempt.

"When God gave the word to Moses to stretch out his staff, the hail came down from the sky amid loud thundering, and a strange fire ran along the ground everywhere, except in Goshen where we Hebrews resided. Any person or animal out in the open died from the plague. In addition, the crops in the field that had come up were severely damaged or burned. As Egypt was being brought to its knees by the plague of hail, Pharaoh and his priests continued to cry out to

Set and Nut. They put food offerings before their statues in the palace and bowed before them. But the hail, thunder, and fire continued unabated. Chastened, Pharaoh sent for Moses and Aaron. Pharaoh said, 'I have sinned. Your God is just, but I and my people are wicked. Pray to the Lord to stop the hail and thundering, and I will let you go.'

"Moses agreed to do so after he was outside of the city. However, once the hail and thunder stopped, Pharaoh went back on his word and instructed his officers to prevent the Hebrews from leaving.

"The next day, Moses and Aaron returned to Pharaoh, as directed by God. Moses said, 'The Lord says how long will you refuse to bow down to Me? Let my people go so they may worship Me, or tomorrow, I will bring locusts throughout your borders. They will cover the land and eat whatever remained after the hail.' With that, Moses and Aaron left the palace grounds.

"Pharaoh's officials immediately begged him to let the Hebrews go. 'Egypt is being broken! How much more devastation can we endure? Let them go to serve their God! Haven't you yet figured out that Egypt has been destroyed by all of these plagues?'

"So, Pharaoh relented and ordered that Moses and Aaron be brought back to him. When Moses and Aaron arrived for their audience with

Pharaoh, the Pharaoh initially seemed conciliatory. Pharaoh said, 'You may go, but who will be going?'

"Moses responded, 'Everyone, of course, our wives and children with us and our cattle."

"But Pharaoh said, 'No! Only the men may go!' Then, turning to his guards and officials, Pharaoh said, 'Now get them out of here!' With that, they were pushed and hustled out of the presence of the pharaoh.

"Once outside the palace grounds, God instructed Moses to stretch his staff out over Egypt to summon the plague of locusts. Moses, therefore, raised his staff. A stiff, steady wind began to blow, but there were no locusts immediately. However, after the wind blew all night, in the morning, such a horde of locusts had blown in that they covered the ground everywhere except in Goshen. There had been locust swarms before, but nothing of this magnitude. There were so many that they almost blocked out the sun. The locusts ate everything in the fields and on the trees left from the plague of hail. Not one green thing was left.

"Pharaoh and his priests appealed to a statue of the god Osiris, the Egyptian god they believed was responsible for the fertility of crops. All the while, all green plant life was being munched away by the plague of locusts. Finally, Pharaoh urgently sent for Moses and Aaron.

When they arrived, he came down from his throne in the great hall and said to Moses, 'I have sinned against your God and against you. Once again, please ask your God to take away this plague.'

"Moses and Aaron left without a word. Once outside, Moses asked Yahweh to remove the locusts. Yahweh heard Moses and granted his request. A strong wind began to blow. This time, rather than bringing in more locusts, it swept the locusts out of the country so that by morning, there was not one locust to be seen, but the devastation from them was everywhere. Yet, after this supernatural display, Pharaoh still refused to let us Hebrews go.

"I don't understand," said Ephraim, "Why didn't Yahweh just let the plagues continue until all of the Egyptians were destroyed and stop giving the Pharoah chance after chance to do the right thing? "

Joshua responded, ' Yahweh is merciful, even to the wicked, and does not want anyone to perish. Yahweh is also patient. He gives the sinner an opportunity to repent, change course, and move in the right direction. Thus, Yahweh told Moses, 'Lift your staff to heaven, and there will come darkness over Egypt so thick that it can be felt.'

"Moses did so, and there was no light for three days, except in Goshen where we Hebrews lived. The thick darkness lasted for three days.

"No Egyptian dared leave the confines of his home. In vain, Pharaoh and his priests made entreaties inside the palace to statues of the sun god Ra, the falconheaded god Horus, and his All-Seeing Eye. But there was no sun for three days, and no one could see.

"After three days of total darkness, Pharaoh again called for Moses and Aaron. After Moses and Aaron arrived, Pharaoh, wishing to seem generous but still in control, said, 'Go ahead and worship your God together with your wives and children, but you have to leave your cattle behind.'

"Moses disputed this with Pharaoh, saying, 'That is unacceptable! We need our livestock to offer sacrifices to God. We will not leave one animal behind!'

"Pharaoh's face turned dark and hard. Looking at Moses, he said, 'Get out of here and don't come back because the next time you see me, you will die!'

"In departing, Moses said, 'Very well. It will be as you say. I will not see your face again. This is what the Lord says, 'About midnight, I will go through the land, and the firstborn son of everyone in Egypt will die from Pharaoh's family to that of the lowest servant girl. The same fate

will be for the cattle.' Moses was angry and let it show. 'When this happens, your officials will bow down to me and beg me to go and the people with me. Then I will go.'

"Pharaoh and his priests went to a statue of the goddess Isis, the goddess that Egyptians believed protected children. They prayed that she would show herself to be mightier than the Hebrew God.

"When he returned to Goshen, Moses told the people to borrow silver, gold, and nice clothing from their Egyptian neighbors. The Egyptians, now terrified, gave them everything they asked for and held nothing back. When I, Joshua, went to borrow from the Egyptians, I was amazed as they loaded me with all of their gold, silver, and fine clothing. Then Moses warned the people to prepare for that evening by killing a lamb for every family. They were to mark their doorposts and lintels with the blood of the slain lamb and stay inside to eat the prepared lamb along with bread free of yeast together with bitter-tasting vegetables. Those who did not obey in offering this sacrifice, sprinkling the blood of the sacrifice, and seeking refuge under that blood covering would experience the death of their firstborn sons just as the Egyptians would. This Passover meal, to be eaten that night, was to be a memorial that would be remembered every year in the future. That night was solemn. My father Nun slew a lamb for us and smeared its blood on our doorpost and

lintels as Moses commanded. As our family ate the roasted lamb, bitter vegetables, and unleavened bread, we huddled together, praying that the death angel would indeed pass over us. I, Joshua, was the firstborn son of my father, Nun. Through the night, I could not help but notice him and my mother looking at me, partly in fear for my life, as we and our Hebrew neighbors could hear in the distance the mournful wailing of the Egyptians as their firstborn males dropped, smitten by the death angel. No one slept that night.

"The next day, Moses left with all of the Hebrew people and their herds. They took with them the precious things they had borrowed from the Egyptians. A few Egyptians, fearing God, aligned themselves with the Hebrews and went with us.

Thus, our numbers included the rabble of a mixed multitude."

CHAPTER 5

Freedom!

"After coming to Egypt 430 years ago as a band of 70 souls, we left Egypt and bitter bondage behind as a multitude of over one million people. (Exodus 12:40-41) Moses took with us the bones of Joseph, which were to be buried in the promised land of Canaan once we took possession of that land. (Exodus 13:19) We moved slowly because most of us walked. Besides, we had our young children and our flocks with us, neither of which could be driven without loss of life. It did not take long for the people to burst out in song. Freedom was in the air!

The Continuing Miracle of the Tangible Presence of God

"Apart from Moses and Aaron, none of us had been outside Egypt. Not only had Yahweh done great miracles to humble the haughty Egyptians and their Pharaoh, but He gave us a daily miracle in the form of His presence as a cloudy pillar to lead us and shelter us from the heat of the sun and at night, a pillar of fire to light the way for us and show us the way through the darkness so that we could also travel by night when it was cooler. (Exodus 13:20-22)

"Our first place of encampment was at Succoth, heading toward Canaan, the promised land. When we departed Succoth on the next day, the manifestation of the presence of God appeared as the pillar of cloud by day and as the pillar of fire at night. From Succoth, it was a relatively short and straight journey to Canaan, the land Yahweh promised to Abraham, Isaac, and Jacob. However, Yahweh's presence in the cloud and fire led us southward to Etham, and from thence we encamped by Pihahiroth between Migdol and the Red Sea. Moses relayed to us the plan of Yahweh. That Pharaoh would think we had gotten lost and become trapped. Yahweh would then harden Pharaoh's heart to come after us with his army thinking of taking back their slaves.

"Sure enough, Pharaoh came at us hard with his army and hundreds of battle chariots. We weren't an army and seemed to be easy prey. Therefore, the people panicked from fear, and some of them got in the faces of Moses and Aaron, saying, 'Did you bring us out here to die because there weren't graves in Egypt? Why did you bring us out here into this wilderness? Leave us alone! We would have been better off as slaves in Egypt than to die here in this wilderness.' (Exodus 14:1-12)

"Moses told the people not to be afraid but to stand still and watch what God would do to the Egyptians because, after this day, they would not

see the Egyptians again. Just stop complaining and hold your peace!

"Yahweh told Moses not to cry to Him, but to tell the people to move forward to the sea, lift up your rod over the sea, and divide the waters so that Israel's descendants cross over on dry ground through the midst of the sea. The cloud of Yahweh's presence moved from before the people to behind them, standing between them and Pharaoh's army while we crossed over. To the Egyptians, it became utterly black. However, for the people Moses led, it provided light. So, the two sides did not come near each other all night.

"As we walked through the sea on dry ground, there was a wall of water on either side of us. I, Joshua, could see fish swimming inside both walls of water. It was an amazing sight. At daybreak, the cloud lifted, and the Egyptians sent their cavalry ahead of their foot soldiers and drove their chariots furiously, including Pharaoh in his royal war chariot, to catch up with the last of us coming up from the sea. Yahweh looked at the Egyptian charioteers and caused the wheels to come off their chariots. The Egyptian foot soldiers, cavalry, and charioteers then feared realizing the God of Israel was fighting against them. Yahweh then commanded Moses to stretch out his hand over the sea again so that the waters would return. Moses did so, and the Egyptians were destroyed by the surging waters of the sea as we watched from a safe place. Not one of the

Egyptian army nor the Pharaoh survived. (Note: "In 1907, when Amenhotep II's mummified body was examined, scientists noticed the presence of unusual [lesions from former boils] all over the body…Evidence of disease would certainly fit with the Biblical account of the plagues.")[5] Yahweh had set a trap for the Egyptians and now we no longer had to be concerned about them or that Pharaoh. When the surging waters receded as the tide pulled back, we were able to quickly go back in from the banks and collect weapons, armor, and shields left over from the Egyptians, who drowned with many of their dead bodies being exposed on the shore. (Exodus 14:28-30) Other than those weapons we collected that day, we had scythes and implements more suited to our work under Pharaoh."

CHAPTER 6

The Victory Song of Moses

"That day, the people feared the LORD and believed the LORD and His servant Moses. (Exodus 14:31) Moses then sang a song to the LORD, and the people repeated it after him, recounting how Yahweh parted the sea for them to pass through to the other side but drowned Pharaoh, his choice of military leaders, chariots, horsemen, and the army of foot soldiers in the sea. Moses went on to sing that fear and dread would come upon the Canaan inhabitants and the leaders of Moab and Edom. Miriam, the sister of Moses, took a timbrel and led the women likewise with timbrels and in dances. (Exodus 15:1-21)

"Moses then led the people, following the presence of the Lord, from the Red Sea out into the wilderness of Shur. After three days in the wilderness without finding a source of water, the people came to Marah but could not drink the water there because it was bitter. The people then complained to Moses, saying, 'What are we going to do for drink?' Moses cried out to Yahweh, and Yahweh directed him to a certain tree. When Moses had that tree thrown into the bitter waters, those same bitter waters became sweet and drinkable. (Exodus 15:22-25)

"The next place the presence of the Lord led us to was Elim. There at Elim were 12 water wells and scores of palm trees. We then camped in that pleasant place. (Exodus 15:27)

"The presence of the Lord then led us to a place between Elim and Sinai known as the wilderness of Sin. There, the people murmured against Moses and Aaron. They said, 'We wish to God we had died in Egypt where we had pots of stewed meat and ate bread until we were full. But you have brought us out into this desert to kill everyone with hunger!' (Exodus 16:1-3)

CHAPTER 7

Bread from Heaven and Water from the Rock

God Provided Even When the People Had a Bad Attitude

"Yahweh heard the people's complaints and considered that their murmurings were not against Moses and Aaron, but against Him, the LORD. Moses relayed to the people Yahweh's words that He would send them bread daily, except for the seventh day, which they were to keep as a Sabbath. Each person was to gather a tenth of a bushel and twice as much on the sixth day. They were to eat it all that day except for what they were allowed to keep over for the Sabbath. Those that did not go out in the morning to gather what the people called manna found that it melted away under the sun. Those who went out to gather manna on the seventh day found nothing and went hungry. Those who sought to hoard the manna overnight were shocked to see that it was filled with worms and was rancid the next day. This angered Moses. It was also a simple test from Yahweh to see if the people would be obedient and follow as they were instructed and make the sabbath holy unto the Lord. Moses had Aaron set aside a pot of the

manna to be kept as a memorial. For 40 years, we ate manna until we came to Canaan. (Exodus 16:4-36)

'The presence of the Lord then led us from the wilderness of Sin to Rephidim. We pitched our tents in Rephidim, but there was no water there. Once again, the people took issue with Moses and demanded that he give them water. Moses warned them not to tempt Yahweh with their murmuring and complaints. But the people said, 'Did you bring us out of Egypt to kill us and our children and our cattle with thirst?'

"Moses, therefore, cried out to Yahweh saying, 'What shall I do for these people? They are almost ready to stone me to death!' Yahweh answered by telling Moses to take his rod with him and go before the people, take the leaders of the people from the people, and go to the rock in Horeb. Yahweh told Moses that He would stand before him on the rock. Moses was instructed to strike the rock, and water would come out of the rock for the people to drink. Moses did so with the leaders of the people, who were with him as witnesses. I, Joshua, also, witnessed the miracle. Freshwater burst forth in a torrent from the rock. There was no source for the water other than Yahweh Himself. The miraculous torrent of water immediately dug a pool at the base of the rock, and the overflow from the unending flow of water resulted in a stream that flowed through the camp. Our animals ran to that stream of water

and drank deeply. Children played in the stream of water. Women brought jugs to catch the water straight from the rock. Everyone marveled at the miracle. In the evenings, people would walk by the rock from which the stream flowed to listen to the sound of the water coming forth and to praise Yahweh for His miraculous provision. Moses called that place Massah and Meribah because the people tempted Yahweh, saying, 'Is the LORD with us, or not? The water from the rock and the daily miracle of the manna were constant reminders that Yahweh was indeed with us just as He had been with us in crossing the Red Sea and utterly defeating the Pharaoh and his army by His own hand, which had sought to re-enslave us."

CHAPTER 8

The First Battle and the Rise of Joshua

Joshua Promoted to Field Marshal of the Army of Israel

"At Rephidim, the warriors of the people of Amalek came out against us for battle. (Exodus 17:8) The Amalekites lived near Canaan but were not Canaanites. Amalek was the grandson of Esau, the twin brother of Jacob from whom the people of Israel are descended. Amalek's descendants were the Amalekites, who lived in the desert south of Canaan. We were on a journey to the promised land of Canaan and had no quarrel with the Amalekites nor any desire to displace them from their land. The attack of the Amalekites was unwarranted and treacherous since our peoples were related.

"Moses appointed me, Joshua, to choose out and lead a select force of our men into battle against the Amalekites. (Exodus 17:9) The plan was to engage the Amalekite army the next day. We had never gone into battle before. Rather than take all of our men, some of whom might have been undisciplined in battle, I followed the instructions of Moses and chose out a select force

of those with a stout heart for the battle ahead; besides, we lacked enough weapons to arm all of our men for the fight. As I walked through our tribes, I chose men individually and had them follow me as I continued the selection process. In the end, the group I chose was smaller than the number of the Amalekite warriors that arrayed themselves against us. However, I, Joshua, was confident that Yahweh was with us and that we would prevail.

"The next morning, as I led this select group of our men toward the Amalekite warriors, I gazed up at the hill where Moses said he would be. From that hill, Moses had a clear view of the battle that was about to take place. With him were his brother Aaron and Hur, the husband of Miriam, the prophetess and sister of Moses. Moses held the rod of God in this hand. This was the rod Yahweh used by Moses to bring great plagues on the Egyptians. It was the rod that was stretched over the Red Sea, and Yahweh divided the waters so that we could cross on dry ground. And it was the rod that Moses struck the rock with, at the command of Yahweh, so that water gushed out to meet the needs of our substantial number of people and cattle.

"Once assembled, we marched toward the Amalekite army. Then, we changed to a trot as we grew closer to the Amalekites. When the Amalekites charged toward us, I led our men in a full run toward the Amalekites until we clashed

on the battlefield amidst yells and the sound of bronze weapons striking the same or being parried by shields. We began to put the Amalekite army to the sword, and the screams of their dead and dying filled the air. Our strong arms that formerly carried heavy bricks to build storehouse cities for Pharaoh now rained blows on the Amalekite warriors. I would glance up at the hill where Moses stood with arms outraised over us with the rod of God. All seemed well. My special force of men acquitted themselves well. Then, suddenly, the battle began to turn against us. I wondered why until I looked up at the hill again and saw that the arms of the 80year-old Moses had grown heavy, tired, and were let down. But as soon as he could raise his arms and the staff of God again, the battle returned to our favor. Thus, there began a cycle of the battle flowing, first in our favor and then in favor of the Amalekites, as Moses first raised his arms and then lowered them when his arms became too heavy from the effort. Realizing this, Aaron and Hur, who were on the hill with Moses, put a stone under Moses for him to sit on while they stood on either side of Moses to hold his arms up steady from that morning until the sun began to set. We thus were able to defeat the Amalekites totally. (Exodus 17:11-13) Their survivors threw down their weapons and ran back to the cities of their people. I, Joshua, had our men collect the weapons and armor of the dead Amalekites and

the weapons left behind by those who fled so that we would have more armament for future battles.

"When the battle with the Amalekites was over, Yahweh told Moses to write down what had just transpired in a book to memorialize it and to rehearse it in my ears. This was the first time that Yahweh had a message specifically for me, Joshua. Moses built an altar on that hill and called it Yahweh Nissi; the Lord is our banner. (Exodus 17:14-16)

CHAPTER 9

The Wisdom of Delegation of Authority

Reunion of Moses with His Father in Law

"During the time that the Presence of Yahweh in the pillar of cloud and fire had us camp at the mountain of God, the father-in-law of Moses, Jethro, the priest of Midian, heard of all that Yahweh had done for Moses and for the people Israel. Therefore, Jethro came to Moses and returned to him his wife Zipporah and her two sons, Gershom and Eliezer. (Exodus 18:1-5)

"Moses and Jethro had a pleasant reunion. Moses showed Jethro respect by bowing to him and giving Jethro a welcoming kiss. Inside Moses' tent, Moses gave Jethro the details of all that Yahweh had done to the Pharaoh and the Egyptians for the sake of Israel, God's people. Moses also related the difficulties they encountered and how Yahweh delivered them in every instance. Jethro then praised Yahweh for making him know that Yahweh was greater than all other gods, besting them in the things they had prided in and delivering Moses and the

people of Israel from under the bondage of Pharaoh and the Egyptians. (Exodus 18:7-10)

"Jethro celebrated by making a burnt offering and sacrifices to Yahweh. Aaron and the leaders of the tribes of Israel, including myself, came as witnesses and then sat down to a banquet in honor of Jethro and in thanks to Yahweh. (Exodus 18:11-12)

"The next day, Jethro observed Moses sitting to judge the people's issues. The people stood in line near Moses from morning until evening to present their cases to him. Afterward, Jethro asked Moses why he was doing this by himself from morning until evening. Moses responded that the people came to him so that he could enquire about Yahweh on their behalf and have him instruct them regarding the statutes of Yahweh and His laws. (Exodus 18:13-16)

"Jethro told Moses that what he was doing was not good and would wear him down as well as the people. Jethro then offered his counsel. First, Jethro advised Moses to be the supreme representative and intercessor between the people and Yahweh. In that role, Jethro advised that Moses would bring the significant issues of the people to God and teach the people God's ordinances and laws and how they should walk before Him, and the assignments they needed to fulfill. Second, Jethro advised Moses to select good men to rule over various levels, from rulers of tens to rulers of fifties to rulers of hundreds

and rulers of thousands. In this way, they would bear the burden of ruling with Moses by taking care of issues at their level and only referring to the weightier, harder matters to Moses. Moses listened to his father-in-law Jethro's wise counsel and implemented that before Jethro left to return to his place in Midian." (Exodus 18:17-27)

CHAPTER 10

God Manifests His Presence and Speaks Directly to the People

God Covenants With the People Directly

"Three months after leaving Egypt, the Presence of Yahweh in the pillar of cloud and fire led us from Rephidim to the Sinai desert. There, we pitched out tents near Mount Sinai, the mountain of God. There, Moses went up into the mountain several times. On the first assent, Yahweh called Moses and told him to tell the people of Israel, saying, 'You saw what I did to the Egyptians and how I brought you to Myself as though I had borne you on the wings of an eagle. Now, I present My covenant to you. If you obey My voice and keep My covenant, you will be a peculiar treasure to Me above all peoples of the earth, for the earth is Mine. I will make you to be a kingdom of priests and a holy nation.'

"After Moses came down from the mountain, he called for the leaders of the tribes with the people, which included me, Joshua, and repeated the words that Yahweh gave him to deliver to them. As with one voice, the people said, 'We will do everything Yahweh has spoken.'

"Moses then climbed the mountain a second time and presented the people's response to Yahweh. At that time, Yahweh told Moses that He was going to come upon the mountain in a thick cloud so that the people would hear Him when He speaks to Moses and to them about His covenant. Yahweh also instructed Moses to have the people wash their clothes and sanctify themselves for two days. On the third day, Yahweh would come down on Mount Sinai in their sight. Yahweh also commanded Moses to mark boundaries around the base of the mountain and forbid the people from attempting to go up the mountain at that time because whoever touched the boundary border would be put to death. Whether human or animal, they would not live but be stoned or shot through with arrows to their death. However, when they hear the long blast of a trumpet, they should come near to the mountain.

"Moses came down from the mountain a second time and did all that Yahweh commanded. On the third day, after the people had sanctified themselves, they witnessed a thick smoke on the mountain because Yahweh had come down upon it in fire. The smoke ascended like the smoke of a furnace, the mountain trembled and quaked violently, and the sound of a trumpet grew louder and louder. Moses then led the people near the mountain. The people were terrified. They felt the ground move beneath their feet and could hardly keep their balance as the mountain shook.

"Moses spoke to Yahweh, and Yahweh answered in a voice that the people and I, Joshua, heard. Yahweh told Moses to come up into the mountain again a fourth time. As Moses went up into the mountain, Yahweh spoke to him, saying, 'Go back down and warn the people not to break through to gaze upon Me, which would cause many to die. Also, have the priests that are to come near Me sanctify themselves so that I don't kill them.' Moses responded, 'They can't come up Mount Sinai because You gave us commands concerning the boundaries around the mountain.' Yahweh simply told Moses to go down and return to Him with Aaron but warn the priests and people not to break through so that they are not put to death.

"Again, Moses went back down the mountain to the people to warn them as Yahweh had instructed him. While Moses was at the mountain's base with the people, Yahweh spoke audibly from the mountain for everyone to hear. Yahweh proceeded to identify Himself and to deliver His covenant with its commandments. The people saw the thunder and lightning, heard the blaring sound of the trumpet, and saw the mountain smoking, such that they all backed off a far distance. They pleaded with Moses, saying, 'You should speak to us, and we will listen but don't have Yahweh speak to us, or we might die!'

"I don't understand," said Ephraim. "Why wouldn't the people want to continue hearing the voice of Yahweh directly?"

Joshua responded, "It was because Yahweh's holy presence and voice made them aware of their sinfulness. Moses told the people not to be afraid. He said Yahweh was testing them so that they would be in awe of Him and would not sin.' While the people backed away from the mountain a great distance, Moses, for a fifth time, went back to the thick darkness where Yahweh was. There, Yahweh said to Moses, 'This is what you shall say to the descendants of Israel; You have seen that I spoke with you from heaven.' Then Yahweh reviewed His covenant for the people to abide by, along with many detailed judgments and statutes to live by. Yahweh added, saying, 'Look, I am sending an Angel ahead of you to keep you and your journey and bring you to the place I prepared for you. Take care when dealing with him, and obey what he tells you. Do not make him angry because he will not forgive your sins because he carries My name. But, if you obey his words and do everything I say, I will then be an enemy to your enemies and an adversary to your adversaries. My Angel will go ahead of you and bring you to the Amorites, the Hittites, the Perizzites, the Canaanites, the Hivites, and the Jebusites, and I will cut them off. Do not worship their gods, do not serve them, and don't do the same things that they do. Instead, you are to utterly overthrow them and break down all of

their images of their gods. Serve Adonai, your God, and I will bless your provisions and your water and keep sickness away from your midst.' Yahweh added, 'I will send the fear of Me before you and will destroy all of the peoples that you come to, and I will make your enemies turn their backs and run from you.' Much more Yahweh said, including that the people of Israel would progressively drive out those other peoples and described to Moses what would be the boundaries of the land they would inherit. Yahweh also warned Moses that they were not to make alliances, pacts, or treaties with them or their gods, nor were they to be allowed to live in the land or else they would cause them to sin against Him, and it would be a snare to them.'

"Yahweh then instructed Moses, saying, 'I want you to come up to Me, you, Aaron, his sons Nadab and Abihu, and seventy of the leaders of Israel. That included me, Joshua. Yahweh made it clear that only Moses could come near Him, while the others remained at a distance, and the people should not come up with them.

"Moses went to the people and relayed to them all that Yahweh had said to him for them. The people answered as one, 'We will do everything Yahweh has said. Moses then wrote the words of Yahweh to preserve them. The next day, Moses erected an altar with twelve pillars representing the twelve tribes of Israel and instructed the young men to bring an animal

offering of oxen to each tribe. The blood of each ox peace offering was put in basins. Half of the blood was sprinkled on the altar. Then Moses took the book he had written of Yahweh's covenant and read it aloud before all of the people. Once again, the people responded as one, saying, 'We will do everything Yahweh has said and be obedient. Afterward, Moses took the blood that had been reserved and sprinkled it on the people, saying, 'This is the blood of the covenant that Yahweh has made with you concerning His words I read to you.

Moses then went up into Mount Sinai a sixth time, taking with him Aaron, Aaron's sons Nadab and Abihu, and seventy of the leaders of the tribes, which included me, Joshua. The people were not to follow us. We went up into Mount Sinai together and as we went we were translated into the presence of Yahweh, the God of Israel. Under Yahweh's feet was a pavement of translucent blue sapphire as clear as the heavens. (Exodus 24:10) We saw Yahweh, but He did not place His hand on us. Food was set before us, and we ate and drank, all the while in wonder that we saw Yahweh and did not die. There, Yahweh told Moses to come up into the mountain to receive tables of stone upon which would be the law and commandments written by Yahweh's hand so that Moses could teach them to the people. (Exodus 24:12)

Moses Begins to Use Joshua as His Assistant and Understudy

"We found ourselves back on the mountain just as we were before we were translated into the presence of Yahweh. Moses sent the leaders back to the people with instructions that Aaron and Hur were to tend to matters in his absence. As the leaders went down the mountain back to the people, Moses took me, Joshua, with him further up into the mountain into the cloud that covered the mountain. The glory of Yahweh was there. For six days, Moses and I waited in that cloudy glory without food or drink as we were sustained by the food and drink we had consumed when we were translated into the presence of Yahweh. (Exodus 24:13-16)

"On the seventh day, Yahweh called to Moses from the cloud. Moses went up further into the cloud while I remained behind. Moses was in the cloud with Yahweh for 40 days and 40 nights. Meanwhile, for the people at the base of Mount Sinai, beyond the borders, the glory of Yahweh was like a consuming fire on the summit of the mountain. (Exodus 24:16-18) During that time, Yahweh gave Moses the engraved tables of stone, but He also gave Moses great detail about a tabernacle sanctuary that was to be built using free will offerings from the people. As Yahweh described the intricacies of the design of those things, how they were to be adorned, and the key items that would be in the Tabernacle, He also

called for the making of a gold overlaid ark, what was to be put in it, and how it was to be portered when the tribes moved from place to place. The Tabernacle and the ark were to be a place for Yahweh to dwell in the midst of the tribes of Israel. Moreover, Yahweh said the testimony of the covenant, that is, the tables of stone engraved by His finger, would be placed in the ark with a seat, called the Mercy Seat, capping the ark and adorned with two cherubim of gold facing each other from opposite ends and their wings stretched toward each other covering the Mercy Seat. It was there, in the space above the Mercy Seat, that Yahweh promised to meet with Moses and commune with him about all of the things that He would give as commandments for the people. (Exodus 25:1-22)

"In addition to further detail about the Tabernacle, Yahweh described priestly garments to be worn by Aaron and his sons that they should wear to minister to Yahweh. This included a breastplate and ephod with four rows, each having three precious and semiprecious stones representing the tribes, and two shoulder pieces with two onyx stones engraved with the names of the tribes of Israel, six on one and six on the other. Aaron would wear these special garments and stones to minister before Yahweh in the Tabernacle. Likewise, Aaron's sons were to wear their special garments to assist him in priestly ministry. Yahweh warned that if Aaron or his sons approached His presence without these

priestly garments and stones, they would die because they would bear their own iniquity. (Exodus 28:1-43)

"Yahweh also instructed Moses to publicly consecrate Aaron and his sons before adorning them with the priestly garments and accoutrements. Moses was to offer blood animal sacrifices at that time, and Yahweh would sanctify the Tabernacle and its altar as well as sanctify Aaron and his sons. Then Yahweh promised He would dwell among the descendants of Israel and be their God, saying, 'They will know that I Am Yahweh their God that brought them forth out of Egypt that I might dwell among them for I Am Yahweh their God. (Exodus 29:1-46)

"Yahweh provided other details to Moses about how worship around the Tabernacle was to be conducted. He also commanded Moses to speak to the people to keep the Sabbath as a holy thing and a perpetual part of the covenant. When Yahweh finished instructing Moses on Mount Sinai, He gave Moses two tables of stone, which Yahweh had written on both sides with His finger." (Exodus 31:1-18)

CHAPTER 11

The People Sin Grievously Provoking the Anger of Yahweh and Moses

"Yahweh suddenly told Moses, saying 'Go! Get back down the mountain because your people, which you brought out of Egypt, have voluntarily corrupted themselves in that they have turned away from the way I commanded in My covenant. They have made a molten calf, worshipped it, and offered sacrifices to it, saying, 'These are your gods, Israel, which brought you up out of Egypt.' (Exodus 32:7-8). I have seen that these people are stubborn and contrary. Therefore, stand aside and don't call out to Me so that I may destroy them all with the fire of My wrath. In their place, I will raise up a great nation from you.'

But for the Intercession of Moses, God Would Have Judged the People

"But Moses interceded to Yahweh for the people saying, 'Adonai, why are You ready to release Your wrath against Your people that You brought out of Egypt with mighty deeds? You don't want the Egyptians to say that You brought them out of Egypt with the corrupt intent to kill them in the mountains and wipe them off of the face of the earth, do You? Please turn away from

Your fierce wrath and change Your mind concerning the harm You thought to do to Your people. Remember Your servants Abraham, Isaac, and Israel, to whom You swore by Your own self and told them saying, 'I will multiply your offspring to be as many as the stars of the heavens, and I will give this land that I have promised you unto your offspring to inherit forever.' (Exodus 32:11-13)

"With that entreaty from Moses, Yahweh turned from the harm He thought to do to His people. Moses went from being in the presence of Yahweh and descended Mount Sinai, reuniting with me on the way down. He carried in his arms the tables of stone on which Yahweh had written the covenant on both sides, engraved by His finger. (Exodus 32:14-16)

"As Moses and I, Joshua, neared the base of Mount Sinai, I told Moses, 'I hear people shouting. It must be the sound of warfare from a battle in the camp.' But Moses said, 'It is neither the sound of one side seeking to overcome the other nor of those crying out because they are about to be slain in the battle. Rather, I hear the sound of singing.' (Exodus 32:17-19)

"As soon as we got near the camp, Moses saw the golden calf of the Egyptian god Apsis with the sun disk of the Egyptian god Ra between its horns. Moses saw the people naked, dancing, cavorting, and singing to the idol god. Moses got so angry that he threw the precious tables of

stone from Yahweh down at the base of the mountain such that they broke into many pieces. Moses was filled with rage and with disappointment. For my part, I was stunned. We had just been with Yahweh on Mount Sinai. Moses had communed with Yahweh over 40 days and nights, receiving many details for the worship of Yahweh and keeping the covenant, but the people had utterly turned away and seemed no different than the Canaanites we were to replace. Moses and I had just come from the mountaintop to a pit of sinful behavior contrary to the covenant with Yahweh when He spoke audibly to all the people.

"Moses confronted his brother Aaron, whom he had left in charge, saying, 'Whatever did these people do to you that you have brought this great sin on them?'

"Aaron responded by saying, 'Please don't be angry with me or get hot with rage. You know that these people have their hearts set on mischief. They told me to make them gods that would go before them. 'As for Moses who brought us out of Egypt, we don't know what has become of him.' I then called for them to give me gold. They brought the gold to me, and when I threw it in the fire of the refiner's pot, this calf came out.'

"Aaron certainly lied about his role in the rebellion against Yahweh, including that he was the one that had them strip naked. Seeing the shameful sight of the naked people, Moses went

to the entrance gate of the camp and called out, 'Who is on Yahweh's side? Let him come stand by me.' The men of the tribe of Levi, the tribe of Moses, responded and gathered around Moses. Moses then spoke, saying, 'Yahweh says that each of you should tie his sword on his side and go through the camp from gate to gate, killing every man aligned with the worship of this abominable calf without making an exception for his neighbor or kinsman. Consecrate yourselves to this task today as a service to Yahweh, and you will be blessed.'

"The armed Levite men commissioned by Moses went through the camp as instructed and killed about three thousand men. The sounds of the wounded and dying filled the camp in place of merriment and singing before the calf idol in nakedness. A trail of blood and dead bodies littered the camp.

"The next morning, Moses took the calf idol they had made, burnt it in a fire, grinding it to powder, and spread it on the water, forcing the descendants of Israel to drink it. Moses told the people, saying, 'You have sinned a great sin. Now I will go up to Yahweh; perhaps I can make atonement for your sin.' (Exodus 32:30)

"Moses climbed up the mountain again for a seventh time to the presence of Yahweh and said, 'These people have sinned a big one and made gods out of gold for themselves. Yet please forgive their sin; if not, I pray You would blot me

out of the book You have written in exchange for them.' (Exodus 32:31-32)

"Yahweh answered Moses saying, 'I will blot out of My book whoever sins against me. Now go and lead the people to the place I spoke to you about. Look, My angel will go before you. Nevertheless, when I visit them I will visit the consequences of their sin on them.' Thus, Yahweh sent a plague among the people that killed others, including the women, who had given themselves to the worship of the idol. (Exodus 32:33-35)

"In sending Moses back to the people, Yahweh said, 'I will send an angel ahead of you and drive out the Canaanites, the Amorites, the Hittites, and the Jebusites and bring you into a land flowing with an abundance of milk and honey that I swore to Abraham, Isaac, and Jacob saying 'I will give this to your descendants.' But I will not go into the midst of the people because they are so stubborn and contrary I might destroy them in My wrath as they journey. Also, have them remove their gold ornaments until I decide what to do with them.'

"When the people received Yahweh's message from Moses after he came down from the mountain, they took off their gold ornaments and repented sorrowfully for what they had done."

CHAPTER 12

New Intimacy with God

"Moses pitched a tent outside of the camp at a great distance and called it the tabernacle of the congregation. It was also known as the tent of meeting. Those who sincerely sought Yahweh went to the tabernacle. However, when Moses went there, everyone would get up and stand by their tent doors, watching Moses until he entered the tabernacle. When Moses would enter the tabernacle, the pillar of cloud would descend at the door of the tabernacle, and Yahweh would talk with Moses. The people worshipped Yahweh whenever they saw this.

God Makes Moses and Joshua His Confidants

"Yahweh spoke with Moses as it were face to face, as when a man speaks with his friend. Then Moses would return to the camp. But I, Joshua, who would accompany Moses into the tabernacle, would linger behind in the tabernacle in the presence of Yahweh. (Exodus 33:11) I did so because there is nothing like being in the presence of Yahweh. My whole body and mind were energized by remaining in the presence of Yahweh.

"For all of his intimacy with Yahweh, Moses longed for more, and this pleased Yahweh. On one occasion, while Moses and I were in the Tabernacle of Meeting outside the camp, Moses said to Yahweh, 'You have told me to lead these people, but You have not said who would go with me. You also said that You know me by name and that I have found grace in Your sight. If I have truly found grace in Your sight, show me Your ways so I will know You better, and be certain that I have found grace in Your sight and that these people are Your people.

"Yahweh responded to Moses saying, 'My presence will go with you.'

"To which Moses replied, 'If You don't go with me, then don't have us go any further from this place. And how will other people know that these people and I have found grace in Your sight except that You go with us? In that way, we will be distinct from all other people on earth.'

"Yahweh answered, saying, 'Because you have found favor in My sight, and I know you by name, I will do what you asked for.'

"Moses then asked for more, saying to Yahweh, 'I implore You, show me Your glory! (Exodus 33:18)

"Yahweh responded favorably by saying 'I will make all of My goodness pass before you and as I do I will proclaim My name Yahweh before you and I will be gracious to whom I will be

gracious and I will show mercy on whom I will show mercy. However, you cannot see My face. No man can see My face and live. Look, here is a place by Me. I will have you stand on a rock. When My glory passes by, I will put you in a crevice in the rock and cover you with My hand as I pass by. Thus, you will see My hinder parts, but My face you will not see. (Exodus 33:19-23)

"Yahweh then instructed Moses to chisel out two tables of stone like the former ones that Moses broke. Yahweh promised that He would write the same words on these replacement tables that were on the first set of stone tables. Yahweh also told Moses, saying, 'Get up tomorrow morning and come up into Mount Sinai and present yourself to Me at the top of the mountain.' Yahweh warned that no one could come up with him or be seen on the mountain. Neither were the flocks and herds of the people to come and graze around the mountain. (Exodus 34:1-3)

"Moses did as instructed and chiseled out two tables of stone similar to the former ones. Then, early the next morning, Moses made his eighth assent up on the mountain carrying the two tables of stone. As Yahweh had promised, He descended in the cloud and stood near Moses hiding him in a crevice. As Yahweh passed by Moses, He proclaimed as His own witness, saying, 'Yahweh, Adonai, the merciful and gracious one, longsuffering and overflowing in goodness and truth, having mercy for multitudes of thousands,

forgiving iniquity, transgression, and sin. I will by no means clear the guilty who bear their own guilt and will visit the iniquity of those fathers upon their children and their children's children until the third and fourth generation.'

"Moses got down in reverence, bowing his head to the ground, and worshipped Yahweh. Then Moses petitioned Yahweh, saying, 'If I have found grace in Your sight, my Lord, I pray You, my Lord, go among us and pardon our iniquity and our sin, because we are a stubborn and contrary people, and take us unto Yourself as Your inheritance." (Exodus 34:8-9)

CHAPTER 13

The Covenant Reaffirmed and the Tabernacle Constructed

"Yahweh responded to Moses, saying, "Look, this is the covenant I make. I will do marvelous things in the sight of the people, things that have not been done anywhere on earth, in any nation. All of the people among you shall see the work of Yahweh, for I will do a frightening thing with them. Now, keep My commandments today. If the people do, I will drive out before them the Amorites, the Canaanites, the Hittites, the Perizzites, the Hivites, and the Jebusites. Be careful not to make treaties or pacts with the people of the land where you are going so that it doesn't become a snare to you. Rather, you shall destroy their altars, break their images of their gods, and cut down their groves of trees dedicated as worship spaces to their gods. You shall worship no other god because Yahweh, whose name is Jealous, is a jealous God. So do not make pacts with the people you find in the land so that you go whoring after their gods and sacrifice to their gods, or they call you to eat of their sacrifice, and your sons take their daughters as wives causing them to join them in whoring after their gods. Don't make any molten casts of their gods.' (Exodus 34:10-17)

"There on Mount Sinai, Yahweh again described to Moses the details of the covenant between Him and the people of Israel and the various sacred feasts to be held annually to reaffirm the covenant. Yahweh told Moses to write down the words He had spoken to him concerning the people of Israel because it was His covenant with them and Moses. (Exodus 34:18-27)

"Moses was there on Mount Sinai with Yahweh for 40 days and 40 nights without eating or drinking. The glory of Yahweh sustained him. When Moses came down from Mount Sinai holding the two tables of stone, he did not realize that the skin of his face shown because of his extended time in the glory of Yahweh. Thus, Aaron and the people were afraid to come near him. But Moses beckoned Aaron and the tribal leaders and spoke with them when they approached him. Afterward, Moses had all of the people of Israel come near him so that he could repeat to them all that Yahweh had spoken to him on Mount Sinai. After addressing the throng of people, Moses covered his face with a veil until he went into the tabernacle of the congregation, also known as the tent of meeting. Once inside the tent Moses removed the veil to go before Yahweh there and speak to Him. When he came out of the tent, the people saw his face shining, so Moses put the veil back on and told them the things that Yahweh had commanded. (Exodus 34:28:35)

"Moses instructed the people concerning all that Yahweh had commanded including the details of the new Tabernacle and the priests' garments. He called for an offering to be freely given to supply the Tabernacle and the garments for the priests. The people then left Moses to gather their offerings and returned to him with those same offerings. Moses announced that Yahweh had called by name Bezaleel, the grandson of Hur of the tribe of Judah and Aholiab of the tribe of Dan to do all of the skilled artisan work. To this end, Yahweh filled both Bezaleel and Aholiab with the spirit of God in wisdom, understanding, knowledge, and craftsmanship to design and fabricate in all the various materials of precious stones, gold, wood, and textiles. (Exodus 35:1-35)

"The people joyfully brought so much for the Tabernacle and the priest's garments that Moses had to tell them to cease bringing offerings of materials because they had received more than enough to complete the work. Bezaleel and Aholiab supervised willing, skillful men who assisted them in the work of the sanctuary. For their part, the women wove the textiles needed for the curtains in the Tabernacle and for the priestly garments. At the same time, the skilled men under Bezaleel and Aholiab added the decorative touches of cherubim to the curtains. They also joined ten panels of the curtains into two sections of five each that were then coupled together with loops on the edges for clasps and loops at the top

to hang them. In addition, the tent itself was covered with ram's skins, dyed red, and waterproof skins on the exterior. A scaffolding of brass was made to hold the skins, and wooden planks for the floor were made of hard shittim wood anchored in silver sockets. The floorboards were clad in gold with rings of gold in the floorboards. {Exodus 36:1-38)

"Bezaleel made the Ark, its Mercy Seat, rings for staves, and staves to carry the Ark according to the design and specifications Yahweh had given Moses on Mount Sinai. He used shittim wood overlayed with gold. The rings were cast from gold, and the staves were overlaid with gold. The Ark itself was covered with gold inside and without. The Mercy Seat was crafted of pure gold as were the two cherubim on top of the Mercy Seat. The candlestick of six branches and a central stem was crafted of pure beaten gold. Likewise, the lamps of the candlestick, to hold the oil for light, were made of pure gold. The table for the Tabernacle was made of gold-covered shittim wood. Other sacred implements and an incense altar were also made. The altar of incense was made of shittim wood and covered in gold. Bezaleel also made a holy anointing oil and incense using the standards of an apothecary. (Exodus 37:1-29)

"Bezaleel also made an altar for burnt offerings out of shittim wood and overlaid it with brass. That altar was three cubits high and five

cubits square, with horns on the four corners. Bezaleel also made all of the vessels for the altar, the pots, shovels, basins, fleshhooks, and firepans of brass. He made a brass grate to go under the altar and staves of shittim wood overlaid with brass so the altar could be portered when the camp moved. Bezaleel also made a laver of brass with feet of brass using the brass mirrors that the women donated. For the courtyard leading to the Tabernacle, Bezaleel made pillars with silver filigree, brass sockets, hooks, and fillets of silver and silver caps on top of each pillar. Hung on the pillars was fine twined linen five cubits high. (Exodus 38:1-31)

"Garments were made for the priests, including ephods and breastplates of gold and miters for headgear. The hems of the priestly robes were embroidered with pomegranates and bells. Pants were made for the priests so that their nakedness would not be exposed when they ascended stairs to minister. The priests' clothes were made of fine linen so they would not sweat.

"When all of the work on the Tabernacle, the Ark, all of the major pieces, the utensils, and the priests' garments were completed, they were all brought to Moses. After Moses examined it all to confirm that it was all done according to the designs that Yahweh gave him, he blessed the artisans. (Exodus 39:1-43)

"Yahweh then spoke to Moses, setting a date to erect the Tabernacle and move everything in its place, including the Ark. Moses was instructed to anoint it and the priests at that time and to sanctify it all to Yahweh. Thus, at the appointed time, on the first day of the first month in the second year, the Tabernacle was erected, and sacred furniture and implements moved into their places. Moses placed the tables of stone with Yahweh's commandments inside the Ark, placed the Mercy Seat on top, and had the Ark portered by the gold-covered staves into the Tabernacle, then enclosed it with the curtains. When everything was in its place, Moses, together with Aaron and his sons, washed their hands and feet and entered the Tabernacle, where they washed again at the altar and had the linen boundary hung around the Tabernacle and the courtyard. Thus, this work was completed and dedicated by Moses. But Yahweh came on the scene. A cloud of Yahweh's glory covered the Tabernacle, and His glory filled it. Moses could not enter the Tabernacle at that time because Yahweh's glory filled it, and the cloud of Yahweh's presence that led them rested on the Tabernacle. From that time onward, whenever the cloud of Yahweh's presence lifted above the Tabernacle, the people would break camp and journey to wherever the cloud led them. If the cloud did not lift, they would not journey further until the cloud lifted again. Therefore, the people saw the pillar of cloud on the Tabernacle by day, and it became a

pillar of fire on the Tabernacle by night throughout their journeys until they entered the promised land. In addition, once the Tabernacle was erected and dedicated, Moses and I no longer erected a tent of meeting outside the camp to go there to meet with Yahweh. Instead, the Tabernacle was in the center of the tribes' camps. Moses and I, Joshua, then went to the Tabernacle to meet with Yahweh and hear from Him." (Exodus 40:1-38)

CHAPTER 14

Rituals, Holiness, Remembrances, and Curses

"During the two-year period of time we were encamped at Mount Sinai, also known as Mount Horeb, the cloudy pillar of Yahweh's presence was with us by day, and by night, it became a pillar of fire. We continued to be sustained by the daily miracle of the manna, and the water continued to flow from the rock in quantities sufficient for all of our needs and for our cattle to drink. Moses and I, Joshua, no longer went outside the camp to the tent of meeting, which was no longer erected, but went instead to the Tabernacle of the Congregation. There, in the Tabernacle of the Congregation, Moses and I went regularly. At such times, Moses went behind the veil of curtains to the most holy place where the Ark was located. No candlestick was there, and Moses carried no lamp to light the way. Instead, the glory of Yahweh provided light. Yahweh frequently would speak to Moses from a place above the Mercy Seat on the Ark between the two golden cherubim. Yahweh would speak to Moses, giving him His message to relay to the people. (Leviticus 1:1)

"The first such message from Yahweh to Moses for the people, after the Tabernacle was erected and dedicated, set the protocol for giving offerings to Yahweh in the courtyard of the Tabernacle. These were instructions for the priests and those bringing an animal to the priests or bringing milled fine flour from grain and olive oil for a grain offering. The standards were high. Animals had to be unblemished and healthy. The grain had to be the best of the first harvesting. (Leviticus 1:2 through 3:17)

"Yahweh next spoke to Moses about offerings of atonement for sin for individuals and the people as a whole. These offerings were to be made within the Tabernacle courtyard and before the door of the Tabernacle. This offering of atonement for an individual was for the person who ignorantly, not presumptuously, sinned against Yahweh's commandments. This began with the priest, for how could the priest preside over someone else's offering if he himself had sinned without first bringing a blood sacrifice to cover his own sin? Just as with an individual, if all the people of Israel, through ignorance, had sinned against any of Yahweh's commandments, a blood sacrifice was to be offered for the atonement of the people. In this case, the leaders of the tribes would first have to put their hands on the head of a young bull as being a confession before Yahweh of the sins of the people. Then the priest would kill the bull, taking some of the blood on his finger, sprinkling it as an oblation before

Yahweh, and putting some of that blood on the horns of the altar. The bull's blood would be collected in a basin and poured at the altar's base through the brass grate. However, the bull would be taken out of the camp and burned there as a sin offering for the people.

"If a ruler of the people sins ignorantly, he is to bring a kid goat, without any blemish, to be sacrificed. The ruler is to place his hand on the head of the goat as a confession of his own sin. As with the offering for the people, the priest is to take some of the blood of the sacrifice on his finger and put it on the horns of the altar. As with the bull for the people, the goat's blood is to be collected in a basin and poured out at the altar's base through the brass grate. Likewise, if an individual has sinned ignorantly, he may bring a female kid goat or a female lamb to offer as a sacrifice, as a peace offering to Yahweh. Again, he should lay his hand on the head of the sacrifice before it is slain by the priest. As with the other sacrifices, the priest would take some of the blood on his finger to put it on the horns of the altar. The rest of the blood of the kid or lamb would be collected in a basin and poured at the base of the altar through the brass grate. Thus, that man's sins are forgiven as the priest makes atonement for his sin with the offering.

"If a person sins by touching unclean things so as to defile himself, or swears with an oath, he is to bring a female kid goat or female

lamb as a sin offering. However, if the person is too poor to be able to bring a kid or a lamb, he may bring two doves or two pigeons, one as a sin offering and the other as a burnt offering and the priest will make atonement for him. However, if the person is not able to bring two doves or two pigeons, he should bring the tenth part of a bushel of fine flour to the priest. The priest shall burn part of it as a sin offering on the altar, and the remainder shall be given to the priest.

"Yahweh also told Moses that if a person sins ignorantly by touching the holy things of Yahweh, for his sin, he is to bring an unblemished ram and add silver coins equal to 20 percent of the value of the animal. The silver is to be given to the priest as a sin or trespass offering while the priest atones for him by the sacrifice of the ram.

"Yahweh again spoke to Moses, specifying the trespass offering to be made when someone lies. An unblemished ram shall be brought to the priest, and the priest shall atonement Yahweh with that burnt offering so that the person who lied and did other sins in connection with that lie may have his sin forgiven.

"Yahweh spoke to Moses again concerning the law of burnt offerings and instructed Moses to command Aaron and his sons to follow these instructions. The fire of the altar, which was initially ignited by Yahweh at the dedication of the Tabernacle, was to burn continually. The priest was to lay fresh wood on the fire each morning for

the sacrifices. The fire was never to be extinguished. The censors of the priests were also to use coals from the altar to light the incense in their censors. This was holy, and no substitute was allowed. Burnt offerings were to be laid on the altar. The priests themselves were to wear the priestly garments when doing this service. (Leviticus 6:1-13)

"Aaron's sons were to offer a meal offering of fine flour mixed with frankincense on the altar to be burned, but the remainder, prepared without leaven, was for Aaron and his sons and the sons of their households to eat within the courtyard of the Tabernacle as a holy thing. A separate special meal offering was to be made for Aaron and his sons at the time of being anointed for the priestly service. Half of the portion was to be made in the morning and the remainder in the evening. This offering was to be done perpetually, burnt in a pan on the altar, and not eaten. (Leviticus 6:14-23) Yahweh also told Moses to speak to Aaron and his sons concerning sin offerings. The priests and all of the males of their households were to eat the sin offering in the courtyard of the Tabernacle. However, no sin offering where any blood thereof is brought into the Tabernacle of the Congregation could be eaten. It can only be burnt on the fire of the altar. (Leviticus 6:24-30)

"Moses also relayed to Aaron and his sons the law for guilt or trespass offerings, similar to the sin offerings. In addition, the peace offering was a blood sacrifice accompanied by a meal offering of unleavened fine flour mixed with oil and covered with oil in the form of cakes. But in addition to the unleavened cakes were to be leavened bread. Because these peace offerings were unto Yahweh, no one who was unclean or had defiled themselves by touching something unclean, without having been purified from that uncleanness, could eat of that sacrifice. If such a person did so, they were to be cut off from the people, because that sacrifice pertains to Yahweh. (Leviticus 7:1-21)

"Yahweh spoke to Moses again and told him to tell the people of Israel not to eat any fat from an ox, sheep, or goat. Fat could be used for other purposes but not eaten. And should anyone eat the fat of a beast that has been sacrificed to Yahweh shall be cut off from the people and put out. Likewise, Moses instructed the people not to eat blood, whether of a bird or a beast. Anyone doing so would be cut off from the people and put out. (Leviticus 7:22-27)

"Yahweh commanded Moses to bring Aaron and his sons into the courtyard of the Tabernacle, with the people observing. There, Moses publicly washed them and dressed them in priestly garments. Moses then took the special anointing oil and anointed the Tabernacle and everything

within it. He also anointed all of the holy items in the courtyard of the Tabernacle. Then Moses poured the anointing oil on Aaron's head to sanctify him. After finishing dressing Aaron and his sons, Moses brought a young bull for a sin offering for the priests who placed their hands on its head before Moses killed it. Of that blood, Moses took some on his finger and put it on the horns of the altar to purify it. The remainder of the blood, which was collected in a basin, Moses poured at the base of the altar through the brass grate. Moses also brought a ram for the burnt offering and killed it after Aaron and his sons had placed their hands on its head. That ram was placed on the altar along with the young bull. Moses then brought another ram as the ram of consecration. After Aaron and his sons laid their hands on the head of the ram of consecration, Moses killed it, took blood from it, and put it on Aaron's right ear, right thumb, and the big toe of his right foot. Moses did the same with Aaron's sons. Finally, Moses took the anointing oil and some of the blood on the altar, sprinkled it on Aaron and his garments, and did likewise on Aaron's sons and their priestly garments. Moses commanded Aaron and his sons to eat the meat of the sacrifices together with bread from the basket of consecration before the door of the Tabernacle. What they could not eat was to be burned. Thus, Aaron and his sons had to remain in the courtyard of the Tabernacle for seven days to complete their ordination. (Leviticus 8:1-36)

"On the eighth day, Moses instructed Aaron and his sons to offer offerings for themselves and for the people. This Aaron and his sons did. After that, Moses and Aaron went into the Tabernacle of the Congregation together. When they came out, they blessed the people. When they blessed the people, the glory of Yahweh appeared in the sight of the people. Fire came down from the glory of Yahweh and completely consumed everything on the altar. When all of the people saw that, they shouted unto Yahweh and fell on their faces. From that time forward, the fire on the altar that came from Yahweh was not to be allowed to be extinguished. Each morning, the priests were to bring fresh wood to keep it going for the sacrifices of the day. Also, the incense in the censers of the priests was to be lit using coals from off of the altar from that fire that was initially the result of fire coming from the presence of Yahweh. (Leviticus 8:23-24)

The Swiftness and Severity of God's Judgment and Punishment

"Two of Aaron's sons, Nadab and Abihu, took their censers and lighted the incense in them with fire that did not come from the coals of the ever-burning altar. This displeased Yahweh so much that fire went out from Him and completely burned up Nadab and Abihu. Aaron was stunned and speechless. Moses informed Aaron that this judgment that came upon his sons Nadab and

Abihu was what Yahweh meant when He said, 'I will be sanctified in them that come near Me, and I will be glorified before all of the people.' Aaron kept his silence at this word from Moses. Moses then summoned two cousins of Nadab and Abihu, who were sons of Aaron's uncle Uzziel and told them to carry the remains of Nadab and Abihu outside the camp. Their remains would be treated as so much garbage with no funeral or memorial. Moses then turned to Aaron and his other sons Eleazar and Ithamar, who were all wearing priestly garments and had been sprinkled with the anointing of Moses in their ordination, and severely warned them, saying, 'Don't take the miters off of your heads or tear your garments in grief, or you will die, and Yahweh's wrath will come on all of the people of Israel, but let your Levite tribal members and all of the people of Israel mourn for the fire that came from Yahweh over Nadab and Abihu, but you may not step outside of the area of the door of the Tabernacle in the courtyard, or you too will die, because Yahweh's anointing oil in on you.' Aaron and his remaining sons, Eleazar and Ithamar, listened to Moses and did as he said. (Leviticus 10:1-7)

"Yahweh spoke to Aaron saying, 'Neither you nor your sons should drink wine or any strong drink when you are about to enter the door of the Tabernacle of the Congregation, or you will die. Make this a statute forever through all of your generations of descendants so that they make a difference between what is holy and what is

unholy, and between clean things and things that are unclean, and teach the descendants of Israel all of the statutes I Yahweh have spoken to them through Moses.' (Leviticus 10:8-11)

God Establishes in Detail How People were to Keep Holy

"Yahweh then spoke to Moses and Aaron together, telling them to explain to the people of Israel what they could eat and what was forbidden for them to eat, among mammals, amphibians, lizards, fish, birds, and insects. That is to say, what was to be considered clean to them and what was to be considered unclean to them, saying, 'Because I Am Yahweh your God. Therefore, sanctify yourselves and be holy because I Am holy.' (Leviticus 11:1-47)

"Yahweh spoke to Moses concerning women who bear children. If she gives birth to a male, she is to be unclean for seven days. On the eighth day, the male baby is to be circumcised, and the mother is to continue in purification for 33 more days. If she gives birth to a female baby, she will be unclean for two weeks and then continue in purification for 66 days. In either case, whether she gave birth to a son or daughter, she shall bring an offering to the priest to offer atonement for her that she cleansed because of the blood that came from her. She can bring two doves or pigeons if she is too poor to offer a lamb. (Leviticus 12:1-8)

"Yahweh then spoke to Moses and Aaron concerning the plague of leprosy in a man or woman. Likewise, whether the leprosy is in woven garments of wool or linen or garments of leather or skins. In either case, the person or garment is to be brought to the priest to examine it, quarantine it, and then examine it or the garment again to confirm whether they or the garment is clean or unclean. (Leviticus 13:1-59)

"Yahweh then spoke to Moses, describing the law of how a priest shall declare a person to be clean from leprosy, the offering to be made for the person cleansed, and how the priest is to sprinkle him who is pronounced cleansed from leprosy. Likewise, Yahweh spoke to Moses and Aaron concerning the homes the people would possess when coming into Canaan. Should leprosy be found in the house's walls, a priest would make the definitive determination and take measures to remove stones and make the house clean unless it spreads, and the whole house must be demolished and carted outside of the city. If the house can be saved, the priest shall offer and perform the ceremonial cleansing of the house. (Leviticus 16:157)

"Again, Yahweh spoke to Moses and Aaron together concerning those who have an issue of blood or other bodily fluid, including a menstruating woman or a man who awakes to a discharge of semen. Strict guidelines were to govern their bedding, clothes, and those who were

intimate with them. Requirements were given for bathing and becoming clean again and for burnt offerings. This was so that the people would be separated from what was unclean and that no such unclean person would defile the Tabernacle and die for their error. (Leviticus 15:1-33)

"After Aaron's two sons died for making an unacceptable offering of incense to Yahweh, Yahweh spoke to Moses saying, 'Tell your brother Aaron not to come in an ordinary fashion into the Tabernacle and beyond the veil into the holy place where the Ark and the Mercy Seat are, so that he doesn't die because I will be present in the cloud of glory over the Mercy Seat.' Yahweh explained that once a year, Aaron and the priests after him in the future should make atonement for himself, the Tabernacle, the sanctuary, the priests, and the people. It is to count as a sabbath. (Leviticus 16:1-34)

"Yahweh again spoke to Moses with a message for Aaron and his sons. Sacrifices were to be brought to the priests for sacrifice at the altar in the courtyard of the Tabernacle. In past times, the people of Israel and the foreigners with them offered sacrifices to the devils they had gone whoring after. That shall not be done. Anyone doing so must be cut off and removed from the people. Likewise, if any of the people of Israel or the foreigners among them should eat the blood of any animal, they shall be cut off and expelled from among the people. This is because Yahweh

said, 'The life of the flesh is in the blood, and I have given it to you to pour out at the altar to make atonement for your souls. Therefore, no one of the people of Israel or the foreigners dwelling among you may eat the blood. Whoever does so, whether of the people of Israel or the foreigners dwelling among you, shall be cut off and expelled from among the people. Anyone who hunts and kills a clean beast or clean bird may eat it after first pouring out its blood and covering that blood with dust because the blood is the life of all living things. Therefore, anyone that eats the blood of any creature shall be cut off and expelled from among the people.' (Leviticus 17:1-14)

"At another time, Yahweh spoke to Moses saying, 'Tell the descendants of Israel, I Am Yahweh your God. Do not do the things that the Egyptians did where you used to live. And do not do what the Canaanites do or live according to their ordinances in the land I am giving you. Rather, observe My judgments, keep My ordinances, and live by them because I Am Yahweh, your God.'

"Yahweh also told Moses, saying, 'Tell the people to avoid all types of incest, to avoid adultery and fornication, and do not offer up their young as human sacrifices by fire to the pagan god Molech. Neither should the people engage in same-sex sexual relations or bestiality. These are the things done by the Canaanites that are being put out before you. They defiled the land with

their doings, and their sin was being required of them. But you people of Israel and the foreigners that dwell with you are to keep My statutes and judgments and not do after the manner of the Canaanites so that you do not likewise defile the land and be cast out like the Canaanites before you were cast out. I Am Yahweh your God.' (Leviticus 18:1-30)

"Yahweh spoke to Moses again saying, 'Speak to all of the descendants of Israel and tell them 'Be holy, because I, Yahweh, your God, am holy." Then Yahweh gave Moses various statutes to give to the people to observe. Some restated the ten commandments in the covenant in stone that Yahweh gave to Moses. Once again, the people were reminded not to eat anything with its blood. Prohibition was given again concerning the occult, that is, no magic spells, no reliance on horoscopes to know one's future, do not seek after those with familiar spirits, and do not seek after wizards. Those things defile. Yahweh is your God. Treat the foreigner that lives among you kindly, as one born among you, and love him as you would your own self, because you were once foreigners in Egypt. (Leviticus 19:1-37)

"Again, Yahweh spoke to Moses to tell the people once more that if any of the people of Israel or the foreigners that live among you give their children as a live burnt offering to the idol god Molech, that person should be put to death by stoning. Let them know that I, Yahweh, will be

against anyone who turns a blind eye to anyone who sacrifices his child to Molech without killing him. Likewise, anyone that goes after Molech is like committing whoredom against Yahweh. Yahweh will also be against those who seek after those with familiar spirits or wizards. They shall be cut off and expelled from the people. Yahweh said to Moses, 'Therefore sanctify yourselves and be holy and keep My statutes because I Am Yahweh Mekaddishkem, the God who sanctifies you.' Yahweh went on to tell Moses to forbid the people from engaging in sexual sins like all kinds of incest or bestiality. Put to death by stoning the man or woman who is a wizard or consults with a familiar spirit. They should keep the statutes of Yahweh and not walk in the ways of the Canaanites. Yahweh has called you and separated you from other people so that you are different. Therefore, be holy to Yahweh, for you are His. (Leviticus 20:1-27)

"Yahweh spoke to Moses with statutes for the priests, which Moses spoke to the priests and Aaron. These statutes governed who they may marry and how to keep themselves undefiled. Likewise, at the instruction of Yahweh, Moses told Aaron that certain men born to the priestly line could eat of things offered but could not serve as a priest, come near the altar, or venture behind the veil in the Tabernacle if he was blemished or had deformities or was lame so that they don't profane the sanctuaries of Yahweh. (Leviticus 21:1-24)

"Yahweh also spoke to Moses with a message for Aaron and his sons regarding keeping clean so that they do not profane the things of Yahweh. If they become unclean, provision was made for when they might be considered clean again. The unclean, though of the priestly line, cannot eat the holy things offered to Yahweh. Neither can a foreigner eat of the holy things. Yahweh also told Moses the statutes governing how an animal is to be fit for use as a sacrifice. An animal brought to the priest for a sacrifice must be perfect, without blemish, nothing broken, bruised, crushed, maimed, or cut. (Leviticus 22:1-33)

"Yahweh spoke to Moses concerning the feasts of Yahweh, which were to be observed as special sabbaths in addition to the weekly Sabbath. These special feast sabbaths require a burnt offering, a meal offering, a sacrifice, and a drink offering on their appointed annual days. Moses declared these things to the people. Yahweh again spoke to Moses, instructing him to have the people bring pure olive oil so that the seven lamps of the golden candlestick in the Tabernacle would burn continually. Twelve special loaves of bread, sprinkled with frankincense, were to be made weekly and set before Yahweh in the Tabernacle. They were to be eaten by Aaron and his sons. Yahweh also specified the rule of equal amends for offenses to another or cattle of another, including a life for a life when one man kills another. Finally, an

Egyptian-Hebrew son of a Hebrew women fought with another Hebrew in the camp and cursed the name of Yahweh in the process. Yahweh told Moses to tell the people that whoever blasphemes the name of Yahweh should be put to death by stoning. Moses so advised the people and had the man taken out of the camp and stoned to death. (Leviticus 23:1 through 24:23)

"From Mount Sinai, Yahweh spoke to Moses about the law of sabbaths when people come into the promised land. The land itself is to have a sabbath every seventh year without sowing or reaping. Yahweh will cause the land to have a triple harvest in the sixth year so that there will be food in the sixth, seventh, and eighth years. After seven sabbath years of 49 years, the 50th year would be a year of jubilee. Poor Hebrews that sold themselves as a yearly hired servant were to be released, and his children along with him. Likewise, land sold would return to its owner. Thus, the land purchase price would be prorated based on how many years it would benefit the purchaser until it is returned in the jubilee year. Hebrews are not to charge interest for loans to another Hebrew, and Hebrews are not to oppress their Hebrew servants. (Leviticus 25:1-55)

"From Mount Sinai, Yahweh also told Moses that the people should not make idols or craft images to worship them because Yahweh is their God. If the people keep Yahweh's sabbaths, hold the sanctuary in reverence, walk in His

statutes, and keep His commandments, Yahweh, their God, will bless them and the land in every way. There will be peace in their land. Their enemies will flee from them and fall by their swords. Five of them will chase a hundred, and a hundred of them will chase 10,000. But, if the people do not listen to the word of Yahweh, neglect His commandments, and despise His statutes, He will curse them so that they fall before their enemies and be taken captive to a strange land. The land will not give them harvests for their labor, and pestilence and wild animals will come among them. Their images and places of worship to idol gods will be destroyed, and they will be so ravenously hungry under siege that they turn to cannibalism and eat their sons and daughters. Yet, after the land has had its sabbaths, which they had not given if they eventually confess their sin and the sin of their fathers, Yahweh will remember them and His covenant with Jacob, Isaac, and Abraham, and they shall return to their land that He might be their God. (Leviticus 26:1-46)

"Yahweh spoke to Moses concerning those that, of their own free will, vow to offer a thing to Yahweh, whether it be a person, a home, land, or cattle. It would be pleasing to Yahweh. But if that person later wished to buy it back, rules were given to the priest to allow him to do so. However, a person or thing devoted to Yahweh is holy to Yahweh and cannot be sold or bought back. Regarding the firstborn of one's cattle, they

belong to Yahweh, but a person can buy it back with 20 percent added to it." (Leviticus 27:1-34)

CHAPTER 15

After Mount Sinai the Journey to Canaan Resumed

"After being encamped in the wilderness of Sinai for two years in sight of Mount Sinai, Yahweh spoke to Moses and directed him to take a census of the people, counting only males twenty years old and upward. Thus, each tribe was numbered. Joseph was given a double portion; therefore, Ephraim and Manasseh, the sons of Joseph, each were numbered as a tribe to number their descendants. However, the Levities were not counted in the census because Yahweh told Moses they were not to be included in the census because they were devoted to Yahweh and were appointed to the ministry of the Tabernacle of Testimony and over all the things that pertain to it. The Levites were to pitch their tents around the Tabernacle. Theirs, too, was the honor, when the camp was to move, of portering the Ark of the Covenant, taking down the Tabernacle, transporting it, and setting it up again once the cloudy pillar of Yahweh's presence rested at a new campsite. Any foreigner coming near these holy things while the Levites were taking them down, transporting them, and setting them up again was to be put to death. The people were to pitch their tents, by tribe, around the Tabernacle, but after the tents of the Levites. Apart from the

women and children, none of the multitude of foreigners that departed Egypt with them were to be counted in the census. (Numbers 1:1-54)

"Yahweh told Moses and Aaron that the people were to pitch their tents by tribe at a distance from the Tabernacle. On the east side of the Tabernacle, the tribes of Judah, Issachar, and Zebulun were to pitch their tents in that order. To the south of the Tabernacle, the tribes of Reuben, Simeon, and Gad were to pitch their tents. To the west of the Tabernacle, there was to be the tribe of Ephraim, and next to that tribe, Manasseh and Benjamin, in that order. On the north side of the Tabernacle, the tribe of Dan was to camp, and next to that tribe, Asher and Naphtali. (Numbers 2:134)

"Yahweh spoke to Moses to count the number of male Levites from age one month and upwards according to their three lines of descent, Gershon, Kohath, and Merari. They were to be devoted to Yahweh and serve Aaron and his sons in all things related to the Tabernacle. The Gershonites were to encamp behind the Tabernacle on its west side and be in charge of the Tabernacle tent, its coverings, the hangings for the door of the Tabernacle, and the courtyard of the Tabernacle. The descendants of Kohath were to encamp on the south side of the Tabernacle and have the honor of portering the Ark of the Covenant, the table for the bread, the golden candlestick, the altars, and the sanctuary

vessels. The descendants of Merari were to encamp north of the Tabernacle. They were to be in charge of the floorboards of the Tabernacle, the bars and sockets that connected them, and the pillars of the courtyard, including their sockets, pins, and cords. On the east side of the Tabernacle, it is to be reserved for the tents of Moses, Aaron, and Aaron's sons. Any foreigner coming near was to be put to death. (Numbers 3:1-39)

"Yahweh then told Moses to number all of the firstborn males from one month old and upwards. A poll tax of five shekels was to be collected for each firstborn male and given to Aaron and his sons to redeem them. Except for the Levite firstborn males because Yahweh was taking them for Himself. (Numbers 3:40-51)

"Yahweh told Moses and Aaron that when the camp moves to follow the presence of God leading them in the pillar of cloud, it was to be the Kohaths of Levi of ages 30 years old and above that were to cover the Ark, the table of showbread, all of the holy vessels and implements, the altar, and the candlestick and its lamps, and porter them to the next campsite under pain of death should anyone actually touch the holy things. Meanwhile, Aaron's son Eleazar was to oversee the Tabernacle overall and the things in it. He was also to be responsible for the oil for the lamps, anointing oil, incense, and the meat offering.

"Yahweh also spoke with Moses and Aaron further concerning the Kohathites. When approaching the holy things, they should not look at those things without them being covered or they would die.

"Again, Yahweh spoke to Moses to count the men of Gershon aged 30 years and upward. Their service would be to porter the curtains of the Tabernacle, the badger skins, and the Tabernacle door hangings. Aaron's son, Ithamar, would be over them. Regarding the descendants of Merari, aged 30 years to 50 years old, they were to be in charge of the planks of the floor of the Tabernacle, their bars, sockets, pins, cords, and pillars. (Numbers 4:1-33)

"Yahweh then spoke to Moses to instruct the people to put any person with leprosy outside of the camp in quarantine. Also, any wife suspected of adultery was to be tested and proved by water mingled with dust from the floor of the Tabernacle. The results, after she drank it, would either vindicate her with pregnancy by her husband or curse her with manifestations in her belly and genitals. (Numbers 5:1-31)

"Yahweh again spoke to Moses, giving him the procedures for a man or woman who wanted to separate themselves for a time under a Nazarite vow. Moses relayed that information to the people and the priests. Then Yahweh told Moses, saying, 'Tell Aaron and his sons to bless the descendants of Israel with these words, 'May Yahweh bless you

and keep you. May Yahweh cause His face to shine on you and be gracious to you. May Yahweh lift up His countenance over you and give you peace.' Thus, they shall put My name on the descendants of Israel, and I will bless them.' (Numbers 6:22-27)

"When Moses had set up the Tabernacle, anointed, and sanctified it and all of the implements, vessels, and the altar, the princes of the tribes brought offerings of silver, covered wagons, and oxen to pull the wagons. All of these offerings were given to the Levites by Moses to the Levite descendants of Gershon and Merai to transport the things of the Tabernacle and courtyard when the camp would move. However, wagons and oxen were not given to the descendants of Kohath because their service was to port the sacred things of the sanctuary on their shoulders. (Numbers 7:1-9) After the altar was dedicated, Moses went into the Tabernacle and behind the curtain to the Ark of the Covenant. There, Moses heard Yahweh speak to him from between the two cherubim on the Mercy Seat over the Ark, and Moses spoke to Yahweh. (Numbers 7:89)

"Yahweh spoke with Moses and gave instructions for Aaron concerning lighting the lamps of the golden candlestick. Again, Yahweh spoke to Moses concerning the Levites. He instructed that the Levites be separated from the other descendants of Israel. They were to shave

their entire bodies and wash themselves and their clothing. Moses was to present them to the people and purify them with burnt offerings. The people themselves were to put their hands on the Levites, and Aaron was to offer the Levites before the Lord as an offering to all of the people to do Yahweh's service. Yahweh made it clear that the Levites were His, and He was giving them to Aaron and his sons after an atonement offering for them to serve in the things of the Tabernacle. Only those Levite males from age 25 to 50 years were to serve. (Numbers 8:1-26)

"Yahweh spoke to Moses and instructed him to have the people of Israel mark the Passover unto Yahweh annually with a feast. When the Tabernacle was set up and dedicated, the cloudy pillar of the presence of Yahweh covered the tent of the Tabernacle and appeared as fire through the night. After two years encamped at the base of Mount Sinai, where they received abundant water from the rock that Moses struck and split, they were about to resume their journey to the promised land of Canaan. Whenever the cloud lifted, they would break camp and journey until the cloud stopped and rested over the Tabernacle, whether for a few days for a few months, or as much as a year. (Numbers 9:1-23)

"Yahweh spoke to Moses, instructing him to make two silver trumpets to signal when the whole camp was to move and when the tribal leaders were to assemble before Moses and to

sound an alarm. In the second year since leaving Egypt and encamping around Mount Sinai, the cloud of the presence of Yahweh lifted up from the Tabernacle, and the people began their journey from Sinai to Canaan. When the pillar of cloud lifted, Moses would say, 'Let Yahweh arise and His enemies be scattered. Let them that hate You flee before You.' When the pillar of cloud came back down to rest on the Tabernacle, Moses would say, 'Return Oh Yahweh to the multiplied thousands of Israel.'" (Numbers 10:1-36)

CHAPTER 16

Complaints, Criticism, Rebellion, and Nonbelief

God and Moses Are Exasperated by the People Repeatedly

"No sooner had the journey to Canaan been resumed and the presence of Yahweh led the people away from Mount Sinai and the clear, refreshing water gushing from the rock, the people began to complain. Yahweh heard them, and His anger became hot against them, so much so that a fire from Yahweh burnt up those on the edges of the camp. These were primarily the non-Hebrews that left Egypt with them. When the people came crying to Moses for relief, Moses prayed to Yahweh, and the fire ceased. Unfortunately, the people did not learn from that incident. The non-Hebrews that fled Egypt with them started talking about the food they had left behind in Egypt, namely the cucumbers, melons, leeks, onions, and garlic. This infected the Hebrews, too, and they longed for those things they ate in Egypt. They complained to Moses that they were tired of eating the manna and wanted some meat. Moses heard lament in unthankfulness for the daily miracle of the manna and whining for meat. Yahweh's anger

began to rise again, and Moses was not happy either.

"Moses began to complain himself to Yahweh because he was depressed by the people's demands. Moses found it too much to bear. Moses spoke to Yahweh, saying, 'Where am I supposed to get meat for these people? They keep crying to me, saying, 'Give us meat to eat!' This is too much for me to bear. If you don't intend to change this situation, then just kill me. It will be a kindness so that I don't have to see how wretched my lot has become.

The Institution of Seventy Elders Established by God

"Yahweh then told Moses to bring 70 men from the leaders of the tribes of Israel to Him and have them stand with you next to the Tabernacle of the congregation. And Yahweh said, 'I will come down and talk with you there and take some of the spirit that is on you and put it on them; thus, they will bear the burdens of the people with you so that you don't have to do it alone. And tell the people to sanctify themselves because you will eat meat tomorrow. You will eat meat because you said you had it better in Egypt. For this reason, I, Yahweh, will give you meat to eat. Not for one day, two days, neither 10 days, or 20 days, but for a whole month until it begins to come out of your nostrils and you loathe it. Because you have despised Yahweh, who is among you, and you

wept before Me saying, 'Why did we ever leave Egypt?'

"Moses responded to Yahweh, saying, 'These people will be 600,000 men ready for battle, not counting women and children. You said You would give them meat to eat for a month. Shall we kill all of our flocks and herds for them, or shall we pull in all of the fish in the sea to satisfy them all?'

"Yahweh answered Moses saying, 'Has My hand become short? You will now see whether My word will prove true to you or not.'

"Moses went out and told the people what Yahweh said, gathered 70 tribal leaders, and arrayed them around the Tabernacle. Then Yahweh came down in a cloud and took some of the spirit that was on Moses and gave it to the 70 tribal leaders. Once that spirit rested on them, they all began to prophesy without ceasing. Two of the 70 were not at the Tabernacle but remained in the camp. Nevertheless, they were too prophesied, but they were in the camp. When a young man came running to Moses, he informed him that two of the tribal leaders were prophesying in the camp. At that moment, I, Joshua, being among the 70, said, 'Moses, my lord, tell them to stop!'

"Moses looked at me and said, 'Are you envious for my sake? I would to God that all of Yahweh's people were prophets and that Yahweh would put His spirit on them.'

"Then a wind from Yahweh brought in quails from over the sea that brought them low over the camp two cubits off the ground, not only filling the camp but for a day's journey any direction from the camp. The people gathered quail all day and all night, and all the next day, they gathered the quail. When those who had lusted for the meat put it in their mouths, and before they could even begin to chew, Yahweh struck them with a plague, and they died. (Numbers 11:1-35)

"When Moses married an Ethiopian woman, Aaron and Miriam openly criticized him, saying, 'Has Yahweh only spoken to Moses? Hasn't He also spoken to us?' This angered Yahweh such that He immediately spoke to Moses, his brother Aaron, the high priest, and Miriam, the sister of Moses, instructing the three to meet Him at the Tabernacle. Once they arrived, Yahweh came down to the door of the Tabernacle in a pillar of cloud and called Aaron and Miriam. When they stepped toward the door of the Tabernacle, Yahweh spoke, saying, 'Listen to what I am saying. When there is a prophet among you, I Yahweh will visit him in a vision and will speak to him in a dream. With My servant Moses, I will speak mouth to mouth, clearly, and not in riddles. He will see My form. So how is it that you two were not afraid to speak against My servant Moses?'

"After speaking thus to Aaron and Miriam, Yahweh's anger burned against them, and He departed as the cloud of Yahweh's presence lifted up from the Tabernacle. As it did, they recognized that Miriam was leprous. Aaron begged Moses to reverse the curse of leprosy on Miriam and admitted to their sin in challenging Moses' leadership.

"Moses called out to Yahweh to heal Miriam in that instant. But Yahweh spoke to Moses, saying, 'If her father had just spit in her face, wouldn't she bear that shame for seven days? Put her out of the camp for seven days. After that she can be received back in again.' Accordingly, Miriam was put out of the camp alone for seven days. During that time, the encampment stayed put at Hazeroth before moving on to the wilderness of Paran. (Numbers 12:1-16)

Canaan is Spied Out with Dire Consequences for a Negative Report

"At Paran, Yahweh told Moses to send 12 men, each a prince of his tribe, to spy out the land of Canaan. I, Joshua, was among the twelve as prince of the tribe of Ephraim. At that time, Moses changed my name from Oshea to Jehoshua. Only the tribe of Levi was not represented because Levi belonged to Yahweh while Joseph had a double portion with a prince each from Ephraim and Manasseh.

"We went up from the south. Around Hebron, we saw Anak's offspring. At Eshcol, we cut down one cluster of grapes that was so large and heavy that it took two of us to carry it on a staff. We also picked some pomegranates and figs to take back with us. After 40 days, we returned to the camp of Israel, presented ourselves to Moses, Aaron, and all the people, and showed them the fruit we brought back. We spies were in accord with our report that the land flowed with milk and honey. However, 10 of our fellow spies gave a bad report, saying, 'Although the land is good, the people there are too strong for us. They live in great walled cities, and the descendants of Anak the giant are among them.'

"Caleb, the prince of Judah, motioned to still the people who were dismayed by the report of 10 of our fellow spies. He said, 'Let's go up right now and take the land to possess it because we are well able to overcome any obstacles.'

However, the 10 spies who had received the negative report argued that we were not able to go up against people who were stronger than us. Besides, they said, 'We saw giants, the offspring of Anak, that are of the race of giants. We looked at them and we seemed to be like grasshoppers in our sight, and we looked like grasshoppers to them too.' (Numbers 13:1-32)

"With such a bad report from 10 of the spies, the people wept in despair that night and turned against Moses and Aaron, saying, 'Would

to God we had died in Egypt or died in this wilderness. Why did Yahweh bring us to this land to be slain by the sword and have our wives and children taken captive? Wouldn't we better off to return to Egypt?' The people then agreed among themselves to select new leaders to replace Moses and Aaron and return to Egypt. With this mutiny, Moses and Aaron fell on their faces before all the people.

"I, Joshua, and Caleb tore our clothes, and we appealed to the people of Israel, saying 'The land we passed through is exceedingly good. If Yahweh delights in us, He will bring us into the land and give it to us, a land flowing with milk and honey. Only do not rebel against Yahweh nor fear the people of that land. They will be like bread for us. Their defenses will not save them. Yahweh is with us, so don't fear them.'

"Instead of listening to me and Caleb, the people shouted that they should stone us to death. They would have done so except the glory of Yahweh appeared in the Tabernacle in the sight of all of the people. Then Yahweh said to Moses, 'How long will these people provoke Me, and how long will it be before they believe Me after having seen all of the signs I have shown among them? I will strike them down with a pestilence and disinherit them. In their place, I will make from you a greater and mightier nation than they are.'

"But Moses interceded for the people before Yahweh saying, 'If You do this, the Egyptians will

hear about it and tell other nations that this was the people that You were among with Your presence standing over them as a pillar of cloud by day and a pillar of fire by night. If You kill them all at once, then the other nations that had heard of Your fame will say it is because Yahweh wasn't able to bring them into the land He swore He would give them. Please remember what You said to me when You said, 'I am Yahweh, and I am long-suffering, of great mercy, forgiving iniquity and transgressions, and by no means clearing the guilty, visiting the iniquity of the fathers upon the children to the third and fourth generation.' Therefore, pardon, I plead to You the iniquity of this people according to Your great mercy, just as You have forgiven them from when we left Egypt until now.'

"Yahweh listened to Moses and granted his petition saying, 'I have pardoned them according to your request. However, because those men who saw My glory on Mount Sinai, and the miracles I did in Egypt and in the wilderness, yet have tested Me now 10 times, but have not obeyed My voice, none of them will see the land I swore to give to your ancestors. None of those who have provoked Me will see it except My servant Caleb because he had a different spirit and followed Me wholeheartedly. I will bring him into the land, and his descendants will possess it.'

"Then Yahweh added these words saying to Moses, 'Tomorrow turn back into the wilderness

along the Red Sea.' Yahweh also spoke to Moses and Aaron, saying, 'How long shall I put up with this evil congregation that murmurs against me? I have heard them that murmur against Me. Tell them, as truly as I live, I will do to you the very words you have spoken. Everyone 20 years and older who murmured against me will not come into the land I swore to give, except for Caleb and Joshua. Your carcasses will fall in the wilderness. But your little ones, that you said would be a prey, those are the ones I will bring into the land. Your children shall wander in the wilderness for 40 years while your carcasses fall in the wilderness. They shall wander in the wilderness one year for each day that the spies took to check out the land. A year for a day.'

"The 10 spies of the princes of the tribes of Israel died suddenly of a plague before Yahweh. Only Caleb and I, Joshua, remained standing among the 12 spies. (Numbers 14:1-38)

"The people were grieved over the things Yahweh said about them to Moses and the death of the 10 princes who were spies that brought back the negative report that caused them to rebel. As a result, they got up early the next morning and advised Moses they would take on the Canaanites and confessed their sin in doubting Yahweh and rebelling. Moses told them to attempt that now would add sin to sin and lead to their defeat because Yahweh would not be with them. Moreover, I would not go with them to lead

them. Moses warned them that the Amalekites and Canaanites would resist them and cut them down by the sword because Yahweh would not be with them seeing they had already turned their backs on Yahweh. Still, they presumed to attack the hill where the Amalekites and the Canaanites dwelt. Moses did not go with them, and the Ark of the Covenant remained in the center of the camp. I, Joshua, remained by the side of Moses and refused to go up with the unauthorized force. As Moses had warned, the Amalekites and Canaanites defeated the contingent that came against them and chased them off. (Numbers 14:39-45)

"After that farce, Yahweh spoke to Moses and told him to tell the people about the sacrifices they should make to Yahweh when they finally come into the promised land. The same would apply to the foreigners who traveled with them. The same laws would apply to the foreigners among them as to the Hebrews.

"While they were still in the wilderness, a man caught gathering sticks on the sabbath was caught and brought to Moses and Aaron in a gathering of the whole congregation to see what should be done. Yahweh spoke to Moses, calling for the whole congregation to stone that man to death outside the camp, and they did as they were instructed.

"Yahweh then spoke to Moses to have the descendants of Israel add fringes to the borders

of their garments and add a blue ribbon upon those fringes as a way to remember Yahweh's commandments, from generation to generation, and do those commandments rather than go like whores after other gods or the unlawful desires of their hearts. Yahweh said, 'They shall be holy to Me, and remember that I am Yahweh, who brought them out of Egypt to be their God. Yes, I am Yahweh, their God.' (Numbers 15; 1-41)

A Mutinous Conspiracy Challenges Moses and is Uniquely Judged

"Nevertheless, the seeds of rebellion against Yahweh and His chosen leaders, Moses and Aaron, continued to manifest. Korah, a Levite of the line of Kohath, along with Dathan, Abiram, and On of the tribe of Reuben, gathered like-minded men together with them, including 250 princes that were of notable reputations, to confront Moses and Aaron, saying 'You have elevated yourselves and taken on too much power since every one of the congregation of the people is holy and Yahweh is with us all. Why then do you presume to put yourselves over Yahweh's congregation?'

"When he heard these words, Moses fell on his face and spoke to Korah and the company with him saying, 'Tomorrow Yahweh will show those who are His and who is holy and will only allow those whom He has chosen to approach Him. Do this in preparation: bring your censers,

Korah, and all of your company, and put fire in them to light your incense. Those whom Yahweh has chosen will be the holy ones. You descendants of Levi have presumed too much. Now Korah and you descendants of Levi, do you think it was of little consequence that Yahweh separated the Levites from the rest of the congregation of Israel to come near Him to perform the service of the Tabernacle of Yahweh and to present yourselves to the congregation to minister to them? And now you dare to seek the priesthood, too? Know that you and all of your company have come together against Yahweh. And what offense has Aaron done that you murmur and conspire against him?'

"Moses had them send for Dathan and Abiram, who were part of the conspiracy, but they refused to present themselves at Moses' command. Rather, Dathan and Abiram sent back a rebellious response to Moses, saying, 'You think it is a petty thing that you brought us up out of Egypt, a land that flowed with milk and honey, to kill us in the wilderness unless we make you a prince over us? Besides, you haven't brought us into a land that flows with milk and honey or given us fields and vineyards as an inheritance. Do you intend to gouge out our eyes? No! We won't come to you.' (Numbers 16:1-14)

"This made Moses incredibly angry. He said to Yahweh, 'Don't accept their offering. I have not taken so much as one ass from them, nor have I

hurt any of them.' Then, turning to Korah, Moses said, 'You and your company be here tomorrow, all 250 of you with your censers.'

"On the next day, Korah showed up with his 250 conspirators. They put fire in their censers, put incense in with the fire, and gathered the congregation roundabout as they stood before the door of the Tabernacle before Moses and Aaron. And Yahweh spoke to Moses and Aaron, saying, 'Get away from this congregation so I can kill them all in an instant.'

"But Moses and Aaron fell on their faces and interceded for the people saying, 'Oh God, the God of the spirits of all humankind, will You be angry with all of the people of the congregation of Israel because of one man's sin?'

"Yahweh spoke to Moses again saying, 'Speak to the congregation and tell them to get away from the tents of Korah, Dathan, and Abiram.'

"Moses got up and went to the tents of Dathan and Abiram with the leaders of Israel following behind him. Moses pleaded with the people, saying, 'Get away from the tents of these wicked men and don't touch anything that pertains to them so that you, too, are not consumed in the judgment of their sins.'

"The people backed away from the tents of Korah, Dathan, and Abiram all around on every side. Dathan and Abiram came out in front of

their tents with their wives, sons, and little children. Moses then said, 'This is how you will know that Yahweh has sent me to do all of these works because I have not done them on my own based on my own thoughts. If they die a death that is common to all men or a common circumstance befalls them, then Yahweh did not send me. But if Yahweh does something new and the earth opens up and swallows them and they go down quickly into the pit, then you will know that these men provoked Yahweh.'

"Once Moses finished speaking, the ground opened up and swallowed all of the conspirators, including their tents and all their things, and they went down alive into the pit screaming, and the earth closed back up on them. All of the congregation that witnessed this ran away when they heard the conspirators and their families screaming for fear they, too, would be swallowed up. As for the 250 men that were before the Tabernacle, fire came down from Yahweh and utterly consumed them, leaving only their censers.

"Yahweh then told Moses to have Eleazar, the son of Aaron, the priest, go and take up those censers out of the ashes because the censers had been made holy. Eleazar was instructed to melt the brass censers of those men down into plates and attach the plates around the altar as a memorial to the people of Israel that no one not of the descendants of Aaron should attempt to

come near the Tabernacle to offer incense to Yahweh that he would not perish as did Korah and the company of conspirators with him.

"Nevertheless, on the next day, the congregation of the people gathered themselves against Moses and Aaron, accusing them of having killed Yahweh's people. When they said this the glory of Yahweh appeared over the Tabernacle and the cloud covered it. Moses and Aaron approached the Tabernacle, and Yahweh spoke to them, saying, 'Get away from these people so I can kill them all in an instant.'

"Moses and Aaron fell on their faces before the Tabernacle and Yahweh's presence to intercede for the people. Moses then told Aaron to take a censer, put fire from the altar in it, and then add incense and run among the people to make atonement for them because Yahweh's wrath had already gone out from Him in a deathly plague. Aaron did as he was instructed to make atonement for the people and he stood between the living and the dead. The plague was stopped, but not before 14,700 people died in addition to those that had died from the conspiracy and rebellion of Korah. Aaron returned to Moses at the door of the Tabernacle, and the plague was stopped. (Numbers 16:15-50) "Yahweh then spoke to Moses to have all of the princes come together with a rod representing their tribe with Aaron brining a rod to represent the tribe of Levi. There were 12 rods in all. Each prince was

instructed to carve his name on his rod. Yahweh instructed Moses to gather the 12 rods and place them in the Tabernacle. Only the man chosen by Yahweh would see his rod blossom. With this sign, they would know who it was that was chosen by Yahweh.

"Moses relayed Yahweh's words to the people, collected the rods of the tribal princes and placed them in the Tabernacle. On the morning of the following day he saw that Aaron's rod, representing the tribe of Levi, had both budded, had some blossoms, and also yielded some almonds. Moses brought all of the rods out of the Tabernacle and had each prince collect the rod on which he had inscribed his name. But Yahweh told Moses to take Aaron's rod that budded and place it with the Ark to be kept as evidence against the rebels so that they would stop murmuring against Yahweh and Aaron and thus avoid death at the hand of Yahweh.

"The people were afraid and said to Moses 'We are all going to die! Whoever comes near the Tabernacle will die. Are we all to be consigned to death?' (Numbers 17:1-13)

"Yahweh spoke to Aaron with a message for him and his sons, that they would bear the sin of the people and have the tribe of Levi to assist them in their ministry. Neither they nor the Levites assisting them would have any lands as an inheritance in the promised land because Yahweh is their portion. Yahweh instructed

Aaron that the common people were not to come near the Tabernacle so that they would not die, because, if they did so they would be guilty of their own sin and there would be no atonement for them. (Numbers 18:1-32)

"Again, Yahweh spoke to Moses and Aaron concerning a purification ritual with the ashes of a red heifer. In addition, rituals were given to cleanse a person who had become unclean. (Numbers 19:1-22)

"The presence of Yahweh in the cloudy pillar eventually led the congregation to the desert of Zin where they encamped at Kadesh. Miriam, the sister of Moses, died there and was buried there. Since there was no water there the people strove with Moses and Aaron. They said, 'Would to God we had died when our kinfolk (Korah, Dothan, and Abiram) died by Yahweh's hand. Why did you bring us to this wilderness, so that we and our cattle would die of thirst here? Why did you bring us out of Egypt to this forsaken place? There are no seeds here, or figs, or fruit bearing vines, or pomegranates, and besides that there isn't any water to drink.'

"After hearing their complaint, Moses and Aaron turned from them and went to the door of the Tabernacle where they fell on their faces. The glory of Yahweh appeared to Moses and Aaron and spoke to Moses saying 'Take the rod and call the people together. There you shall speak to the

rock and water will come out for them to drink and for their cattle.'

"Moses took the rod, as Yahweh had instructed him to do and gathered the people together saying to them 'Listen you bunch of rebels, do we have to bring forth water for you from this rock?' With that Moses lifted up the rod and struck the rock twice. Water gushed out of the rock in abundance such that the people and their cattle had plenty to drink. This was called the water of Meribah because the descendants of Israel strove with Yahweh.

"However, Yahweh spoke to Moses and Aaron saying, 'Because you didn't believe Me to sanctify Me in the sight of the descendants of Israel, you will not bring this people into the land that I promised to give them.' (Numbers 20:1-13)

CHAPTER 17

Warfare, Treachery, Seduction, Betrayal, and Death

"Moses sent emissaries from their camp in Kadesh to the king of Edom. The people of Israel were related to the Edomites because Esau and Jacob were twin sons of Isaac and Rebecca. The people of Israel sought no conflict with them, just a right of free passage on their way to Canaan. Moses told his emissaries to tell the king of Edom, saying, 'You know what has befallen us, your relatives. Our ancestors went down to Egypt, and we stayed there for a long time, but the Egyptians troubled our ancestors. We cried to Yahweh, and He heard us. He sent an angel and brought us out of Egypt. We are encamped in Kadesh, a city beyond your border. We pray that you would allow us to pass through your country. We won't trample your fields or go through your vineyards. We won't even drink from your wells. We will keep to the king's highway and won't deviate from it either to the right or to the left until we have passed beyond your borders.'

"Nevertheless, the king of Edom answered by saying, 'Don't try to pass through my domain, or I will come against you with the sword on the field of battle.'

"Moses's messengers countered by saying, 'We will keep to the highway, and if any of our cattle drink any of your water, we will pay for it. We would only request passage via the highway and nothing more.'

"But the king of Edom answered harshly, saying "You will not go through.' Then, the king of Edom sent his warriors to the border with Kadesh and refused to grant passage to the people of Israel. Because of this, the camp of Israel turned away from Edom and, instead, went from Kadesh to Mount Hor. (Numbers 20:14-22)

"After the whole congregation decamped from Kadesh and were led by the presence of Yahweh to Mount Hor, Yahweh spoke to Moses and Aaron saying, 'Aaron shall now go the way of his ancestors who died before him and shall not enter into the land I have given to the descendants of Israel because the two of you rebelled against My word at the water of Meribah. Now take Aaron and his son Eleazar and bring them with you to Mount Hor. There, Moses, you are to strip Aaron of his priestly garments and dress Eleazar, his son, with them. When you do, Aaron will die there and join his ancestors.'

"Moses did as Yahweh had instructed, and Aaron fell down dead at the top of the mountain. Moses and Eleazar, the new high priest, came down from the mountain with Aaron's body. When the people in the camp saw that Aaron was dead, they mourned for him for 30 days. (Numbers 20:14-29)

Miriam, the visiting young girl, asked, "Why did Aaron die like that?"

Joshua replied, 'There were three things that Aaron did that displeased Yahweh. First, while Moses was in Mount Sinai receiving the covenant from Yahweh, Aaron gave in to the people and made a golden idol representing Apis and Ra as the gods that brought them out of Egypt. Second, Aaron and Miriam challenged Moses for leadership. Miriam was immediately judged with a plague of leprosy and put outside the camp for seven days. Nothing happened to Aaron at that time because he was in the office of the high priest. Third, Moses and Aaron dishonored the word of Yahweh at the water of Meribah when Moses got angry and struck the rock rather than speaking to it as Yahweh had instructed. Aaron's judgment was delayed because of his position as the high priest. The time was then near to enter Canaan, and Aaron was the last of the older generation under the curse of Yahweh when the people heeded the negative report of the 10 princes who spied out Canaan with me and Caleb. Yahweh said they would not enter into the land.

"When King Arad of the Canaanites in the south heard that the people of Israel were coming by the route south of the Dead Sea that the spies of Moses used to spy out Canaan, his warriors fought with the army of Israel and took some prisoner. The people of Israel vowed to Yahweh,

saying, 'If You deliver these people to us, we will utterly destroy their cities.'

"Yahweh heard them and delivered those Canaanites into their hands. The people of Israel, under my leadership on the battlefield, then utterly destroyed them and their cities and called the name of that place Hormah. After that, we were led by the cloudy pillar of the presence of Yahweh back to Mount Hor and around the borders of Edom along the Red Sea. It was a rough journey, and the people began to complain against Yahweh and against Moses, saying, 'Why did you bring us out of Egypt to die in this wilderness? There is no food or water here, and we are sick of this manna.'

The People Insult God and His Provision of Manna, Reaping the Consequences

"Yahweh was displeased with their complaints and sent fiery serpents among the people. When the serpents bit the people, they experienced agonizing pain like the pain of being burnt by fire. Many people died from those serpents. Therefore, the people came to Moses and confessed their sin of complaining against Yahweh and against him and begged Moses to get rid of the serpents. Moses prayed for them.

"Yahweh listened to Moses's prayer for the people and told Moses, saying, 'Make a fiery serpent and put it on a pole. Whenever someone

is bitten, if he looks on it, he will live.' Moses made a serpent of brass and set it up on a pole as Yahweh had directed. Just as Yahweh had said, if a person were bitten but looked upon the brass serpent on the pole, he lived.

"Following the cloudy pillar of the presence of Yahweh, the people encamped in several different places until they came to Beer. At Beer, Yahweh spoke to Moses to gather the people together to a certain place where He would give them water. As the princes of the tribes dug with their staves at the place Moses indicated, the people sang, 'Spring up, oh well', and water sprang up like a continuous geyser to provide all of the water they needed. (Numbers 21:4-18)

Joshua Leads the Conquest of the Lands West of the Jordan River

"From there, the presence of Yahweh in the cloudy pillar led them to several places that they camped in succession in the land of Moab and came to Mount Pisgah, also known as Mount Nebo, northeast of the Dead Sea. Moses then sent emissaries to Sihon, the king of the Amorites, saying, 'Let Israel pass through your land. We won't stray into your fields or your vineyards. Neither will we drink water from your wells. Rather, we will journey along the king's highway until we pass beyond your borders.'

"King Sihon, however, would not allow Israel to pass through his domain. Instead, Sihon

assembled his warriors and fought against Israel in the wilderness. I, Joshua, led Israel against Sihon's army, and we put them to the sword and took all of their land and cities and villages of the Amorites up to the border with Ammon. Moses then sent men to spy out Jaazeer, where other Amorites dwelt, and Israel drove out the Amorites from that area, too, under my leadership. (Numbers 21:21-32)

"We then turned northward to Bashan, but King Og of Bashan came out against us with all of his men at Edrei. Yahweh then spoke to Moses, saying, 'Don't be afraid of them. I have already delivered Og and his people into your hands. You will do to them just as you did with King Sihon of the Amorites that dwelt at Heshbon.'

"Again, I, Joshua, led the men of Israel against King Og and his people. We killed Og, his sons, and all of his people until there was no one left alive in Bashan of Og's people. We then took possession of that land. (Numbers 21:33-35)

"We then turned back southward through the land we had already conquered from the Amorites and encamped in the plains of Moab east of the Jordan River and opposite Jericho that was west of the river. Balak, the son of Zippor, was Moab's king, and he was extremely fearful of Israel, having seen what Israel did to the Amorites and the fact that Israel was a large multitude of people. Balak took counsel with the princes of Moab and sent messengers to the prophet

Balaam with his message saying, 'There is a people that has come out of Egypt. They are so many that they cover the earth and are encamped next to me. Come and curse these people for me because they are too strong for me, but with your curse, I can overcome them and drive them out of the land. I know who you bless is blessed, and whoever you curse is cursed.'

"The leaders of Moab went with their allies, the leaders of Midian, carrying payment for the curse they sought from Balaam against Israel. They delivered the message from King Balak, but Balaam told them to wait in his house overnight until he could hear from Yahweh.

"Yahweh appeared to Balaam in a dream and asked, 'Who are these men staying in your house?'

"Balaam responded to Yahweh saying, 'King Balak of Moab sent these men to me saying a people has come out of Egypt covering the earth and asked that I curse them so Moab could overcome them.'

"Yahweh instructed Balaam, saying, 'Don't go with them and don't curse those people because they are blessed.'

"The next morning, Balaam got up and told Balak's princes, saying, 'Go back into your own land because Yahweh will not permit me to go with you.'

"Those princes went back and reported to King Balak that Balaam refused to come with them. Balak responded by sending another delegation to Balaam of higher ranking princes with his message to Balaam saying, 'Don't let anything hinder you from coming to me because I intend to promote you with very high honors and will give you whatever you ask. So come and curse these people for me.'

"But Balaam responded to King Balak's message saying, 'If Balak were to give me his house full of silver and gold, I can't go beyond the word of Yahweh my God, either to do less or more. Just stay with me tonight so I can hear whether Yahweh has anything else to say to me.'

"That night, God came to Balaam in a dream and said, 'If the men ask you to go with them, do so, but only speak the words I give you.'

"In the morning, Balaam saddled his ass and went along with the princes of Moab without even being asked to come with them. God got angry with Balaam as he journeyed and sent an angel to oppose him in the way. The angel blocked the way with a drawn sword in his hand. Balaam's ass saw the angel and veered into the field off of the road to avoid the angel. Balaam got so angry that he roughly beat the animal. Further down the road, vineyards were on one side and a wall on the other. The angel again withstood Balaam. Balaam did not see the angel, but the ass did. To spare Balaam's life, the ass thrust itself

against the wall and, in the process, crushed Balaam's foot against the wall prompting Balaam to beat the ass again. The angel went down the road to another place that was narrow, with no space for the ass to turn aside. When the ass saw the angel at that place, it fell down and refused to proceed. Meanwhile, Balaam took out his staff and beat the ass with something much heavier than the goad he had been using.

"At that point, Yahweh gave voice to the ass, and the ass spoke to Balaam saying, 'What have I done to you that you have beaten me these three times?'

"Balaam spoke back to the ass saying, 'It is because you mocked me. I wish I had a sword in my hand right now because if I did, I would kill you.'

"The ass replied to Balaam, saying, 'Haven't I been your faithful ass that you have ridden for as long as you have owned me. Have I ever done anything like this to you before?'

"Balaam had to respond 'No.'

"At that moment, Yahweh opened Balaam's eyes so that he saw the angel standing before him, blocking the way with a drawn sword in his hand. Whereupon Balaam bowed his head and fell flat on his face over the head and neck of the ass. The angel then spoke to Balaam, saying, 'Why did you beat your ass these three times? I went out to withstand you because you were

pursuing a perverse purpose. The ass saw me and turned from me these three times. If she had not done so, I would surely have killed you by now but saved her life.'

"Balaam responded to the angel saying, 'I have sinned. I didn't know you were in the way to oppose me. Now, if you are displeased, allow me to go back to my home.'

"But the angel said, 'Go with the men, but only speak the words that I speak to you. That is what you are to speak.'

"Balaam then continued along with the princes of Moab. (Numbers 22:1-35)

"When Balaam arrived in Moab, King Balak was happy and went out to meet him. He wanted Balaam to explain why he didn't come the first time he was sent for seeing that he, Balak, was ready to reward him. But Balaam explained, saying, 'I am here with you now, but I am powerless to say anything of my own will. The words that God puts in my mouth are what I will speak.'

"Balak took Balaam the next day to a high place where sacrifices were made to the god Baal. From there, they could see the entire encampment of Israel. Balaam asked for seven altars on which were to be sacrificed: an ox and a ram on each altar. Balaam had Balak stand by those altars while he climbed up to a higher place to meet with Yahweh. While Balaam was in a

trance, God met with him. Balaam showed God the seven altars he set up, but Yahweh put a word in Balaam's mouth, saying, 'Go back to Balak and speak the word I have put in your mouth.'

"When Balaam went back down to King Balak at the altars with all of the princes of Moab gathered around, he spoke the word God put in his mouth saying, 'King Balak of Moab brought me here from Aram out of the mountains of the east saying, 'Come and curse Jacob for me and defy Israel.' But how can I curse those whom God has not cursed? Or how can I defy those whom Yahweh has not defied?' And to the consternation of King Balak, Balaam proceeded to bless Israel. (Numbers 22:36-41 and 23:1-10)

"Balak rebuked Balaam, saying, 'What have you done to me? I brought you to curse my enemies, but you have done nothing but bless them!'

"Balaam answered Balak saying, 'Can I do anything other than speak what Yahweh put in my mouth?'

"Balak then bid Balaam to come to another high place where he would only see part of the encampment of Israel and asked Balaam to curse Israel for him from that place. There, on top of Mount Pisgah, Balak again set up seven altars and sacrificed a young bull and a ram on each altar. Balaam told Balak to stand by the altars

while he would go a distance away to meet with Yahweh.

"Yahweh met with Balaam again while Balaam was in a trance. There, Yahweh put a word in Balaam's mouth and sent him back to Balak to reveal the word. Balak stood with the princes of Moab at the altars and asked Balaam, saying, 'What did Yahweh say to you?'

"Balaam addressed Balak, saying 'God is not a man that He should lie; neither is He the son of man that He should repent and take back His words. Has He said a thing, and won't He do it? Or has He spoken a thing, and won't it come to pass? I received the commandment to bless, and He has blessed. I cannot reverse that. He sees no iniquity in Jacob, nor has He seen perverseness in Israel. Yahweh, his God is with him, and the shout of a king is among them. God brought them out of Egypt, and Israel has, as it were, the strength of a horned dinosaur. There is no enchantment or spell that will succeed against Jacob, and neither is there any divination that can stop him. In time, it will be said of Jacob and of Israel 'What has God wrought!" And with other words Balaam continued to bless Israel. (Numbers 23:11-24)

"Balak was greatly angered and told Balaam, saying, 'Neither curse them in any way nor bless them at all.'

"Balaam protested, saying, 'Didn't I tell you whatever Yahweh speaks I must do?'

"Balak again charged Balaam, saying, 'Come with me to another place. Perhaps it will please God for you to curse them for me from that place.'

"Balak then took Balaam to the top of Peor, where he prepared seven more altars and sacrificed a young bull and a ram on each altar, as Balaam had asked him to do. (Numbers 23:25-30)

"Realizing that Yahweh wanted to bless Israel, Balaam changed his tactic. Instead of seeking a spell of a curse against Israel, he looked at the wilderness where he saw the encampment of Israel arrayed according to their tribes, and the Spirit of God came on him and caused him to speak forth a divine oracle from an open eyed trance saying 'How beautiful are your tents Jacob and your Tabernacle Israel…God has brought you out of Egypt. You have, as it were, the strength of a horned dinosaur. You will consume the nations that are your enemies, breaking their bones and piercing them through with your arrows. You lay down like a great lion. Who dares to stir you up? Blessed is the one that blesses you, and cursed is the one that curses you.'

"Balak was in a fit of rage and beat his hands together before turning to Balaam, saying, 'I called you here to curse my enemies, but you

have blessed them now three times. Go back home. I had intended to promote you to a place of great honor, but Yahweh has kept you back from honor.'

"Balaam replied to Balak, saying, 'Didn't I tell your messengers that if you gave me your house filled with silver and gold, I can't go other than in line with Yahweh's commandment? I can neither do good or evil of my own will, but what Yahweh says is what I speak. I am going back to my home, but first I am going to tell you what this people will do to your people in the end times.' (Numbers 24:1-14)

"Balaam then went into an open-eyed trance and spoke saying, 'I shall see Him, but not now. I shall look upon Him, but not be near to Him. A Star will come out of Jacob, and a Scepter will arise out of Israel and will strike the four corners of Moab and destroy the descendants of Sheth. He will possess Edom and Seir, and Israel will acquit themselves valiantly. Out of the line of Jacob will come Him that will have dominion and will destroy all that remain in the principal city of Moab.' Balaam went on to prophesy against other kingdoms far and near. Then Balaam went back home, and Balak returned to his palace. But Balaam, nevertheless, earned a reward by advising King Balak how he could get Yahweh to turn against Israel by seducing them to sin against Yahweh through fornication with the young women of Moab, eating the meat of animals

sacrificed to Baal and bowing down to strange gods. (Numbers 24:15-25; 31:16, and Revelation 2:14)

"While Israel was encamped at Shittim, Moab and its ally Midian, sent their young women to the tents of Israel to seduce them into fornication, sacrificing to their gods, eating those sacrifices, and worshiping Baal and the other gods of those peoples. This angered Yahweh. Yahweh spoke to Moses, saying cut off the heads of those that joined in with Baal, the sun god of Moab and Midian, and hang them up facing the sun so that My fierce anger can be turned away from Israel.'

"Accordingly, Moses instructed the judges to kill every man that had joined themselves to Baal. While Moses was giving that order, they saw one of the Hebrew men named Zimri, who was a prince of the tribe of Simeon, leading a Midianite woman named Cozbi, the daughter of a principal leader of Midian, to his tent for him and other men to fornicate with her. He did this in sight of Moses and those members of the congregation of Israel who were weeping in repentance at the door of the Tabernacle. Phinehas, the son of Eleazar, the high priest and son of Aaron, when he saw it, left the people who were kneeling at the door of the Tabernacle, took a javelin, and went after that bold man, going into his tent and thrust the two of them through with one stroke as they were fornicating.   That   halted   the   plague   from

spreading further. Even so, 24,000 died from the plague. (Numbers 25:1-9)

"Yahweh spoke to Moses saying, 'Phinehas, the grandson of Aaron and son of Eleazar, has turned My wrath away from Israel so that more were not killed in the plague because of My jealousy. Therefore, I am giving him my covenant of peace and an everlasting priesthood because he was zealous for his God and made atonement for the people of Israel.' Then Yahweh spoke further to Moses, saying, 'Go kill the Midianites because they troubled you with their wiles and led you astray in the matter of Baal of Peor.' (Numbers 25:10-18)

"Yahweh then had Moses number the males aged 20 and above for purposes of dividing to the tribes' land in Canaan for an inheritance. There was not one name found from when Moses and Aaron numbered the men in the wilderness of Sinai. They had all died in the wilderness as God said they would, except for me, Joshua, and Caleb. (Numbers 26:1-65)

"The daughters of Zelophehad of the tribe of Manasseh came to Moses and demanded they be given an inheritance in the promised land because their father died in the wilderness with no male heirs. Moses inquired of Yahweh and was told that what the daughters of Zelophehad said was right and had Moses establish a statute to cover the inheritance rights of women in such a situation.

"Yahweh then spoke to Moses, telling him to go up into the mountain range of Abarim (where Mount Nebo is located). From there, Yahweh would allow him to see the land He had promised to the descendants of Israel. Yahweh added, 'After you see it from the mountains of Abarim, you too will go the way of your ancestors just as your brother Aaron was because you rebelled against My commandment in the desert of Zin, when you strove with the congregation, instead of sanctifying Me at that water in their sight.' (Numbers 27:12-14)

Joshua Selected by God to be Ordained Leader in Place of Moses

"Moses spoke to Yahweh asking Him to select a man out of the congregation to lead them and take them into the promised land so that they won't be like sheep without a shepherd.

"Yahweh answered Moses saying, 'Take Joshua the son of Nun, a man in whom is the spirit, and put your hand on him and set him before Eleazar, the priest in sight of all of the congregation and charge Joshua. You will impart some of your honor on him so that all of the congregation will be obedient to him. Then have Joshua stand before Eleazar, the priest who shall seek counsel from Me for him by the Urim stone before Me, Yahweh.' (Numbers 27:15-23)

"In preparation for the passing of Moses from life to death, Yahweh spoke to him with explicit instructions for the people regarding all of the offerings to be made to Yahweh, especially at the appointed major feasts and convocations. Moses faithfully passed on to the people all that Yahweh had commanded. (Numbers 28:1-31 and 29:1-40)

"Moses assembled the princes of the tribes of Israel and instructed them concerning the issue of vows, including between a man and his wife and between a father and his unmarried daughter still living in his house. (Numbers 30"1-16)

"Yahweh spoke to Moses saying, 'Take revenge, for the sake of the people of Israel, on the Midianites. After that you will die and be gathered to your ancestors.'

"Moses had me, Joshua, take 1,000 fighting men from each of the 12 tribes. Of the Levites, no fighting men were selected. However, Phinehas, the son of Eleazar, the high priest, came with us with other Levites sounding on silver trumpets. We went to war with the Midianites and killed all of their men, including their five kings. The women and children were taken captive together with all of the wealth of the Midianites and their cattle.

"Moses and Eleazar, the high priest, met us, together with the princes of the tribes of

Israel, on the plains of Moab across the Jordan River from Jericho. Moses was angry with the officers and captains of the army, saying, 'You kept all of the women alive? These are the ones that, through the counsel of Balaam, caused Israel to sin against Yahweh in the matter of Baal of Peor. That resulted in a plague in Israel. Now, therefore, do this: kill every male child and kill every woman who is not a virgin. The rest of the female children that are virgins you can keep alive for yourselves.'

"Moses also instructed the victorious armed force to remain outside the encampment for seven days to purify themselves, their captives, and their clothing. Every metallic thing was to be purified by fire, and every other thing was to be purified by the water of purification. Moses also directed the officers and captains to divide the goods and virgin females into two parts. One part was for the men who fought the Midianites, and the other half was for the rest of the people of Israel. But a portion was to be given to Eleazar for an offering to Yahweh, and another portion was to be given to the Levites who take care of the things of the Tabernacle. The officers and captains reported to Moses that after counting their warriors, they found that not one was killed in battle. In thankfulness to Yahweh, they turned over to Moses and Eleazar all of the gold they captured, along with their jewels, to be offered to Yahweh. (Numbers 31:1-54)

Two and One Half Tribes Ask to Remain on Land Conquered West of the Jordan River Outside of the Promised Land of Canaan

"The leaders of the tribes of Reuben and Gad petitioned Moses and Eleazar and the princes of the other tribes asking for the land on the east side of Jordan as their inheritance because they had a lot of cattle and that land was good for cattle raising. Moses was not happy and answered, 'So your brothers are supposed to go to war in Canaan while you sit here? Why would you discourage them from going over to possess the land?' Moses likened their action to the 10 unfaithful spies at Kadesh Barnea, who discouraged the people from entering the land, resulting in 40 years of wandering in the wilderness.

"But the princes of Reuben and Gad drew near to Moses and offered a compromise. They would build sheep enclosures for their cattle and build well defensed cities for their children for their protection, but they themselves would go as an armed force to fight with their brothers to possess the land before they would return on the east of Jordan as their possession. Moses accepted that arrangement for the tribes of Reuben, Gad, and half of the tribe of Manasseh. (Numbers 32:1-42)

"Yahweh spoke to Moses, giving him a command for the descendants of Israel concerning their borders when they come into the land of Canaan to possess it. Moses then relayed that information to the people, saying, 'This is the land that shall be distributed to you to inherit by lot for the nine tribes and to the half-tribe of Manasseh because the tribes of Reuben, Gad, and the half-tribe of Manasseh have received their inheritance, as they requested, on the other side of the Jordan River.'

"Yahweh then spoke to Moses again, instructing him that I, Joshua, and Eleazar, the high priest, would oversee dividing the land among the tribes. Yahweh also gave the name of one prince from each tribe to represent their tribe in this process. No prince was named for the tribes of Reuben and Gad because they had already chosen the lands west of the Jordan River for their inheritance. Also, no one was named for the tribe of Levi because the Levites belonged to Yahweh and would only have a total of 48 designated cities and limited suburbs around those cities for their cattle, beasts, and other goods. Each tribe was to contribute to the total of the 48 cities from their inheritance. In addition, six of the cities would be designated cities of refuge so that anyone who unintentionally commits manslaughter may flee to those cities and be safe from those seeking to avenge the blood of their slain relative. The person committing manslaughter unintentionally must

remain in the city of refuge until judged by the people or until the high priest dies. Three cities of refuge would be on each side of the Jordan River. (Numbers 34:1-29 and 35:1-34)

CHAPTER 18

Farewell Address of Moses, Covenant Reminders, Prophesy, and His Death

Passing the Baton of Leadership and Intimacy with God

"As the time drew near for Moses, who was 120 years old, to die, Moses called all the people together to give them his parting words. Moses recited the history of the tribes from the time Yahweh used him to lead them out of their bondage in Egypt. The vast majority of the people receiving the words of Moses at that time were not even born until after God used Moses to bring the people out of bondage in Egypt through great signs and wonders. Apart from Moses, Caleb, and myself, Joshua, there was not one person older than 60 years old because the older generations died in the wilderness, as God said they would when they first refused to go into the land of Canaan out of fear from the negative report of 10 of the 12 spies Moses had sent to spy out the land over a 40-day period.

"These words Moses spoke to the gathered tribes on the west side of Jordan. He reminded all of how their parents and grandparents doubted Yahweh and His promise, fearing to go into the promised land and possess it. For that reason, only Caleb of that generation would go in to possess the land, and his descendants would inherit the land because Caleb followed Yahweh wholeheartedly. As for me, Joshua, Moses said I should take them into the land. He called on the people to encourage me in this because I would cause Israel to inherit the land. However, nothing was said of my descendants because I did not marry and had no children. Moses himself would not get to go into the land because, in his anger with the people, he struck the rock with his rod a second time in disobedience to Yahweh. (Deuteronomy 1:21-38)

Mariam asked, "Why didn't you marry and have children?"

Joshua replied, "As the servant of Moses, I went up Mount Sinai with him. I was translated into the presence of Yahweh along with Moses and the elders. In addition, I accompanied Moses into the tent of meeting to hear from Yahweh in His presence. I even stayed behind in the presence of Yahweh after Moses left the tent of meeting. There is nothing like the presence of Yahweh. It far exceeds the love of a woman. Besides, Yahweh did not ask me to marry and raise children.

"Moses recounted how, after wandering in the desert for 40 years until the doubting generation that came out of Egypt died off, Yahweh sent them up west of the Jordan River but would not allow them to go to certain places. Only as we were attacked did we fight against and defeat those kingdoms on that side of Jordan that fought against us or schemed to get us to anger Yahweh by sinning against Him. We fought and overcame those kingdoms even though they had cities fenced about with high walls, gates, and bars, such as in Bashan, in addition to the many unwalled towns. (Deuteronomy 2:2-37 and 3:1-17) When the tribes of Reuben, Gad, and the half-tribe of Manasseh asked to take that land as their inheritance, Moses granted their request, provided they would go into the promised land on the other side of Jordan and fight to help the other tribes possess that land, which they agreed to do. (Deuteronomy 3:18-20)

Moses Reaffirmed God Had Chosen Joshua to Lead the People into the Promised Land

"Moses reminded the people that Yahweh had chosen me, Joshua, to succeed him. Also, even though Yahweh would not allow him, that is, Moses, to enter the promised land and commanded him in anger not to raise the matter again, Yahweh had Moses go to the top of Mount Pisgah to look westward, southward, and northward to see the land as a bird would see it

as it flew over the land. Then Yahweh instructed Moses to charge me, Joshua, to take the people of Israel into the promised land to inherit it. (Deuteronomy 3:21-28)

"Then Moses rehearsed to the people of Israel how Yahweh had chosen him to give his laws and statutes to the people so that they would keep the covenant between them and Yahweh and not do as the people they were displacing had done with images and idol gods Yahweh had forbidden. Yahweh is a jealous God. Moses went on to warn the people of the dire things that would happen to them if they broke the covenant. But Yahweh is also a merciful God. Moses prophesied how Yahweh would deliver them from those things once their descendants remember the covenant, turn from serving idol gods, and seek Yahweh once again with their whole hearts and souls. (Deuteronomy 4:1-31)

Moses Rehearsed What God Had Done for the People

"Moses reminded the people of the great wonders Yahweh performed to deliver them from their Egyptian bondage and how they were unique of all nations for how Yahweh dealt with them, even speaking to them with a voice they could all hear audibly. Accordingly, Moses again cited the details of the covenant, especially the Ten Commandments, including all of the

commandments, statutes, and judgments. (Deuteronomy 5:1-33 and 6:1-25)

"Moses made plain how they were to deal with the peoples they would displace and destroy all vestiges of their worship of idol gods. He also reminded them of how quickly they had forsaken Yahweh and built and worshipped a golden calf idol while he was on Mount Sinai, receiving the tables of stone with the covenant. Yahweh would have even killed Aaron for his part in the betrayal, but Moses interceded for the people and for Aaron, pleading for Yahweh to remember his promises to Abraham, Isaac, and Jacob. (Deuteronomy 9:1-29)

Choose the Blessings of God's Covenant or Choose the Curse

"Moses presented the people of Israel with two options. One option was the blessings of Yahweh if they kept the covenant. The other option was a terrible curse if they chose not to keep the covenant and obey the commandments and statutes but instead reject Yahweh and serve the idol gods of the Canaanites. (Deuteronomy 11:13-32 and 12:1-32)

"Moses told the people that Yahweh would raise up a prophet like him from among them, and that they should listen to that prophet." (Deuteronomy 18: 15-19)

Miriam asked, "Was Moses referring to you when he said that?"

Joshua replied, "No. Moses was not referring to me, but was speaking instead of the Messiah. Yahweh told the serpent in the Garden of Eden that the seed of the woman would strike his head and he, meaning Satan, would strike his heel. (Genesis 3:15) In addition, the prophesy that Yahweh forced the perverse prophet Balaam to speak said a star would come out of Jacob that would be a scepter rising out of Israel. Balaam also said, he saw him, but it was not for time in the near future. (Numbers 24:17) Also, when Jacob prophesied over his sons before his death, he spoke of the scepter coming out of Judah, but I am from the tribe of Ephraim. (Genesis 49:10) Yahweh appointed me, but I am not that Messiah, even though Yahweh was with me as He was with Moses.

"To prepare the people for the combat to come on the other side of the Jordan River, Moses encouraged the people not to be afraid of their enemies, their military resources, or the number of warriors at their disposal because God would be with them and He would fight against their enemies to save His people Israel. (Deuteronomy 20:1-4)

"Regarding the Canaanite kingdoms, which were the Hittites, Amorites, Canaanites, Perizzites, Hivites, and the Jebusites, they were all to be destroyed. Only those kingdoms that

were much further removed could be offered terms of peace; otherwise, they, too, could be dealt with as enemies, sparing only their women and children. (Deuteronomy 20:10-18)

"After instructing the people as to how they were to comport themselves when they come into the land of promise, Moses specified the many ways in which they would be blessed if they would listen to God's voice and keep all of His commandments. However, if they did not listen to God's voice and would not keep the commandments and statutes that Moses gave from Yahweh, terrible curses were prophesied against them. (Deuteronomy 28:1-68)

"Finally, Moses said to all of the people of Israel that he was 120 years old, and Yahweh had told him he would not cross over the Jordan River. But I, Joshua, would go over with them. Moses encouraged us to be courageous and not be fearful because Yahweh would go with us. Then Moses called for me in the sight of all Israel and charged me, Joshua, to be strong and courageous because I was the one who would lead the people, and Yahweh would go before me. (Deuteronomy 31:1-13)

"Yahweh then spoke to Moses after these things and told him to take me, Joshua, with him into the Tabernacle because Moses would soon die, and Yahweh wanted to give me His charge. Prior to this, only Moses was allowed to go into the holiest part of the Tabernacle where the Ark

rested, other than when the camp moved or when the high priest would enter once annually. We then went and entered the Tabernacle. There, Yahweh appeared in a pillar of cloud. That pillar of cloud also appeared over the door of the Tabernacle. Yahweh spoke from the space between the Mercy Seat and the wings of the cherubim on top of the Mercy Seat. Yahweh again told Moses that he was about to die and gave him a prophecy about the future of the people of Israel. Yahweh said that after the death of Moses, the people would go after idol gods and break the covenant He had made with them, causing Him, Yahweh, to turn from them, which would result in many calamities befalling them. Yahweh then had Moses write down a song given to him to instruct the people. (Deuteronomy 31:14-22)

"As for me, Joshua, Yahweh spoke to me and said, 'Be strong and have good courage because you will bring the descendants of Israel into the land that I swore I would give them. And I will be with you.' (Deuteronomy 31:23)

Author and spouse at the Franciscan marker stone on Mount Nebo

"Moses then had the Levites gather the tribal leaders. Once gathered, Moses spoke to them the words of the prophetic song about Israel's future that Yahweh had given him for the people. After giving the song to the people that same day, Yahweh told Moses to go up to Mount

Nebo, which was across the River Jordan from Jericho, where he was to die but be able to see the promised land of Canaan and what would be the next step that I, Joshua, would take the people. (Deuteronomy 31:28-30 and 32:1-52)

Lookout point from Mount Nebo where Moses possibly stood. The marker evokes both a crucifix and the brass serpent of Moses. The map on a stand to the left indicates how close cities and landmarks in what was Canaan are to Mount Nebo.

"Before Moses went up to the summit of Mount Nebo to die, he blessed the tribes individually, including Levi, and combined Ephraim and Manasseh under Joseph. Before Moses gave up his life, Yahweh allowed him to see all of the promised land. Then Yahweh buried the

body of Moses in a valley near Beth Peor in what had been the land of Moab. However, no one knows where that gravesite actually is, so the people would not make it a memorial. Moses was 120 years old at the time of his death. When he died, his eyesight was strong, and he had the physical strength of a much younger man. For 30 days, the people of Israel wept and mourned the passing of Moses. However, they did look to me, Joshua, because Moses had laid his hands on me at my public ordination as his successor and imparted some of the spirit that Yahweh had placed on him to me, just as Yahweh had done the same in imparting some of the spirit that was on Moses to the 70 elders of Israel to share the burden of judging the people. Therefore, the people listened to me." (Deuteronomy 33 and 34)

The view from the summit of Mount Nebo to the Dead Sea (center left), where the Jordan River empties into the Dead Sea, is likely where Joshua led the nation of three million souls across the river. In the distance (center background) are Jericho and Jerusalem.

CHAPTER 19

The Transition to Life Without Moses

God Again Gives Joshua His Charge and His Pledge to Be With Him

"After the 30-day mourning period, Yahweh spoke to me, Joshua, saying, 'My servant Moses is dead. Get up now and cross this Jordan River, you and all of these people, and go into the land that I have given them, to them the descendants of Israel. I have given you every place the sole of your feet treads. As I told Moses, the land extends from the wilderness to Lebanon and from the Great Sea to the Euphrates River. No man will be able to stand up to you as long as you live. I will be with you just as I was with Moses. I will not fail you, and I will not desert you. Therefore, be strong and keep your courage up. You will divide the land among the people as an inheritance, the inheritance that I swore to their ancestors that I would give them. Only be strong and very courageous so that you keep all of the laws that My servant Moses commanded you to keep. Do not deviate from it either to the right hand or to the left so that you succeed wherever you go. The book of the law should always be in your mouth. Meditate on it day and night so that you observe

and do all that is written in it. Then you will cause your efforts to prosper, and you will have good success. Haven't I commanded you to be strong and courageous? Do not be afraid, and don't get your head down because Yahweh, your God, is with you wherever you go.' (Joshua 1:1-9)

"After Yahweh spoke to me following the death of Moses and the end of the mourning period I and all of the people observed, I, Joshua, called together the leaders of the tribes and commanded them to have their people prepare food for several days because we would cross the Jordan River and begin to possess the land that Yahweh had already given us. I also charged the men of the tribes of Reuben, Gad, and the half-tribe of Manasseh to fight at the forefront to assist their brothers of the other tribes to gain their inheritance while their own wives, children, and cattle remain in the land Moses agreed to give them for their inheritance west of the Jordan River. All of the tribal leaders pledged, saying, 'We will do whatever you command. Where you send us, we will go. Just as we listened to Moses in every matter, we will listen to you. We ask that Yahweh, your God, would be with you just as He was with Moses. Anyone rebelling against your commands will be put to death. We ask that you be strong and courageous.' (Joshua 1:10-18) We all noted that the Jordan River was at flood stage during that waiting time. Being without boats and there being no bridge, we all wondered how we, as a multitude with children and cattle, would ford the river.

"Before embarking on our campaign to possess the land, I sent two men to spy out the land of our crossing, especially the city of Jericho. They went and boarded into an inn belonging to a prostitute named Rahab. But the king of Jericho became aware from reports brought to him that men from Israel were amongst them as spies. That king sent men to Rahab, demanding she bring out the men who had come to her. But Rahab hid them on her roof under piles of flax stalks and told the king's men that they had already departed, encouraging the king's men to pursue them beyond the city gate in hopes of overtaking them. Before Rahab hid my two men, she told them that she knew Yahweh had given Israel the land, and she revealed that the terror of Israel was on them and made them weak. Rahab recounted that they had heard how Yahweh had dried a path in the Red Sea for the people of Israel to leave Egypt. They also knew how Israel had utterly destroyed the Amorite kings on the other side of the Jordan River. Rahab acknowledged that Yahweh is God of heaven and earth. She asked for her life and the lives of her parents, sisters, brothers, and their children. Our spies told her to put a scarlet cord from her window on the city wall as a sign to spare those in her house when Jericho would be taken. For her part, she let them down from her window at night and advised them to go and hide in a certain mountain until after the king's men returned to the city after failing to capture them. (Joshua 2:1-22)

"When my two spies returned, they reported to me saying, 'Yahweh has most certainly delivered the land into our hands because all of the inhabitants of that country are fainting for fear of us.' They also advised me of how Rahab had protected them and to whom they had pledged, in turn, to spare her life and the lives of her near family that would gather in her house. (Joshua 2:23-24)

"When the time came to cross the Jordan River and invade the land of Canaan, I, Joshua, commanded the people saying, 'Sanctify yourselves because Yahweh will do miraculous wonders among you tomorrow.'

God Promises to Do Miracles for Joshua as Evidence He is with Him

"Yahweh also spoke to me saying, 'Today I will begin to make you great in the eyes of all of Israel so that they will know that I will be with you just as I was with Moses.' (Joshua 3:7)

"I relayed to the people Yahweh's instruction that the priests were to bear the Ark of the Covenant ahead of the people and step out into the water but remain there until the floodtide waters coming down from the north piled up in a heap, leaving dry land for the people to cross over. In this way, they would know that God is among them and would drive out at their head the Canaanites, Hittites, Hivites, Perizzites, Girgashites, Amorites, and the Jebusites. And it was so until everyone had crossed over. (Joshua

3:9-17) After everyone had crossed over and a man from each of the 12 tribes collected stones from the riverbed to erect a memorial on the Canaan side of the river, the priests with the Ark came over too, at my command, following Yahweh's word to me, and the waters again flowed freely southward. That day, Yahweh made me great in the sight of the people so that they feared me as they had feared Moses. (Joshua 3:9-17 and 4:1-18)

"No one had ever seen anything like it before. With fear and dread, they crossed the river as its waters rose higher and higher on their right hand upstream. Although the Jordan River was at flood tide and had overflowed its banks, the water did not go around; it held in place, with the waters coming down from the north piling up against an unseen barrier some distance northward while we crossed over. It was a great miracle demonstrating that Yahweh was with me as He had been with Moses.

"Once everyone, and lastly the priests carrying the Ark, came up out of the dry riverbed of the Jordan, we made camp at Gilgal. There I reminded the people that Yahweh had dried up the waters of the Jordan River until you crossed it, just as He did to the Red Sea when He brought us up out of Egypt. I told them that this was done so that everyone on earth would know that Yahweh's hand is mighty and that you, His people, would be ever in awe of Him.

"When word came to the kings of the Amorites west of the Jordan River, and all of the

kings of the Canaanites dwelling along the Great Sea, that Yahweh had dried up the waters of the Jordan River before us until we had crossed over, they lost all heart. There was no spirit in them to resist us for fear of us. (Joshua 5:1)

"Yahweh then spoke to me to circumcise every male. When we came out of Egypt, all of the men were circumcised, but they died in the wilderness. However, those born in the wilderness as we journeyed for 40 years were not circumcised. I, Joshua, thus made sharp knives and had all of the males circumcised the same day. We then remained at Gilgal and the males in their tents until they had healed and could move freely. Had our enemies not been afraid, they could have attacked and wiped us out because the fighting men would not have been able to defend themselves. But our enemies remained afraid of us and lacked the heart to take us on in battle. (Joshua 5:2-9)

A Major Transition

"While encamped at Gilgal, we observed the Passover in the plains of Jericho at the exact time Moses commanded. However, after Passover, we ate the grain of Canaan. The following day, the daily manna ceased. The quails also ceased. In addition, the sign of Yahweh's presence in the pillar of cloud during the day and as a pillar of fire at night also ceased. These were daily miracles that we had taken for granted for 40 years. Yet because of the crossing of the River Jordan, we knew the God of miracles was still

with us. It was simply different now. (Joshua 5:10-12) No wonder I told the leaders to have their people prepare food in preparation for the crossing. Yahweh had now weaned us off the manna, quails, and the pillar of cloud and fire. We would now take our food from the land and from the stores and cattle of the people we would displace from the land."

CHAPTER 20

The Conquest of the Land of Canaan Begins

Joshua Encounters God the Warrior and is Given the Keys to Taking Jericho

"I, Joshua, walked by myself, surveying Jericho. It was a city on a hill, a high place. In addition, it had thick walls that rose up, which combined to give them some defensive advantages. We conquered the kingdoms east of the Jordan River, including those with walled cities. As I gazed at Jericho, I realized it had defensive advantages such that a smaller force could usually withstand a more considerable force coming against it. I pondered in my mind how to attack this well-situated and defended citadel. We could not shy away from the challenge, but I was unsure how to defeat the city without many of our fighting men getting killed.

Ephraim asked, "Were you afraid of disaster and of the people turning against you should your attack on Jericho result in defeat with many of the men of Israel slain?"

Joshua answered, "I wasn't afraid; I just could not figure out how to successfully take Jericho without an unacceptable loss of life in the effort of our men of war. As I walked near Jericho, strategizing how to take the city, I looked up and saw a man before me with his sword drawn. I approached him and asked, 'Are you on our side, or are you taking part with our adversaries'?

"His response was, 'I am neither. I am here as the Lord of Yahweh's angelic armies.'

"With that, I fell on my face in the dust and worshipped Him as my God. Then I said, 'What does Adonai, my Lord, have to say to me'?

"The Lord of Yahweh's angelic armies replied, 'Take your shoes off your feet because this is holy ground.'

"I quickly complied, knowing that the holy God makes the place where He stands holy, and I was nothing in His sight. (Joshua 5:13-15)

Miriam asked, "Were you afraid of the angel, and was that why you prostrated yourself before him?"

Joshua replied, "No Miriam, I prostrated myself before Him and worshipped Him as my God, because that is who He was. I had a reverential awesome fear of God in whose presence I was. He also did not forbid me to worship Him in this way, because worship is due Him. No mere angel of Yahweh would dare take

God's glory and seek or accept worship that belongs only to Yahweh. (Joshua 5: 13-15)

"At that time, Jericho was shut up as though it was under siege. No one went into it, and no one came out of it. As I lay prostrate on the ground with my face in the dust and my shoes off before Yahweh Sabaoth, the Lord of Heaven's armies, He spoke to me saying, 'I have given Jericho, its king, and its mightiest warriors into your hand. You shall march around the city with your warriors once daily for six days. The priests shall go after the warriors bearing the Ark and having seven ram's horn trumpets. On the seventh day, you shall march around the city seven times, after which the priests shall blow the trumpets. When they make a long blast with the ram's horn trumpets, everyone shall shout with a great shout. Then the walls of the city shall fall down flat. Your warriors shall then each ascend up into the city.' (Joshua 6:1-5)

"I, Joshua, commanded the people saying, 'Neither shout nor make any noise from your mouths and don't speak a word until the day and time I tell you to do so, then you shall shout."

"For six days, we assembled early each morning to march around Jericho. The well-armed warriors were in the lead, followed by the priests carrying the Ark of the Lord and other priests blowing on the ram's horn trumpets. Behind them was a rearguard of other armed men of Israel. Each day, we saw the archers and

catapults on top of the city walls, but we were beyond the reach of their arrows and large stones. Each day for six days, I could see the red cord hanging from the window on the wall where Rahab dwelt. We had prepared no ladders or machines of war to scale the walls. Yahweh Sabaoth had already told me the walls would fall out flat on the seventh day once the priests made a loud, long blast with the ram's horn trumpets and the people lifted up a loud shout as a war cry. Then, the walls falling out flat would be ramps for our warriors to go up into the city and take it.

"On the seventh day, after we had marched around the city seven times, I, Joshua, gave the signal saying, 'Shout! Because Yahweh has given you the city!' I also commanded our warriors to spare Rahab and everyone in her house because she hid the men we had sent. I warned everyone that Jericho was cursed and everything in it. Therefore, they were not to take anything for themselves so that they would not be cursed and bring a curse on the camp of Israel. But all of the silver, gold, and vessels of brass and iron were to be consecrated to Yahweh and entered into the treasury of Yahweh.' (Joshua 6:6-19)

"After I gave the signal to shout, the priests gave a long blast on the ram's horn trumpets, and the people let out a loud shout. Then the walls of Jericho rumbled and fell out and down flat, enabling our men of war to go straight up into the city. There they killed men, women, the young

and the old, and all animals, too; oxen, sheep, and asses were put to the sword. I dispatched the two men I had sent as spies to go to Rahab's house and bring out safely Rahab and all her family there with her to keep the pledge they had sworn to her. Thus, Rahab and her family were brought out safely but were required to live outside the camp of Israel. When our men of war completed their work in the city, they put it to the torch and burned what remained. I sealed it by pronouncing a curse over Jericho. (Joshua 6:20-26)

Remains of the walls of ancient Jericho. ID 118857651 (c) Mikhail

Semenov Dreamstime.com

"After we took Jericho, some days after Yahweh dried up the Jordan River for our crossing, my fame was spoken of throughout all of Canaan. But Yahweh was angry with us because Achan, of the tribe of Judah, had taken from Jericho what was judged to be cursed and taken for himself gold that was to be devoted to Yahweh. But I did not realize this at the time. (Joshua 6:27 and 7:1) Instead, we reveled in our successful campaign against Jericho. Not one man of ours was lost in battle. Some wondered why we didn't take the young women and children captive or save the oxen, sheep, and asses for our own use. There was nothing to explain. This was the first conquest in Canaan, and I made it clear that we were following Yahweh's instructions."

Ruins of the 8th Century AD Islamic Arab Palace of Hisham near modern Jericho

CHAPTER 21

The Price of Disobedience and Presumption

"After the fall of Jericho, I sent men to scout out the town of Ai, which was next to Bethaven east of Bethel. They did so and returned to me with the advice that it was unnecessary to have the entire army of Israel go against such a small town. They suggested sending a force of only two or three thousand men because Ai had only a few people. I listened to them and sent three thousand men to take Ai. But things did not go as planned. The men of Ai routed our warriors, putting them to flight and killing 36 of our men in the process. Then it was us that lost heart. (Joshua 7:2-5)

Joshua Learns Not to Neglect Seeking God's Voice and Direction

"I, Joshua, humbled myself before Yahweh by tearing my garment and laid prostrate before the Ark of the Lord until sundown. Also, both I and the tribes' leaders put dust on our heads. I cried out to Yahweh, saying, 'O Lord God, did you bring us all over the River Jordan only to have the Amorites wipe us out? I wish we had been content to live on the other side of the Jordan River. Since we turned and ran before our enemies, the

Canaanites and all of the other peoples of the land will surround us and annihilate us. What will people say about Your great name then?' (Joshua 7:6-10)

"Then Yahweh said to me, 'Get up! Why are you lying down in the dirt on your face? The problem is Israel has sinned and violated the covenant I commanded them to keep by stealing for themselves things that are cursed and hiding them in their stuff. That is why they could not stand before their enemies, turned their backs, and ran. That is why. And I will not be with these people anymore unless you destroy the cursed thing from among you.' (Joshua 7:11-12)

"Yahweh then instructed me to get up and have the people sanctify themselves and tell them it is because the cursed things have been harbored among them. The next morning, they were to group themselves into tribes. Then Yahweh would show the tribe, clan, family, household, and man that had transgressed. That person, the cursed things, and all that pertains to him, his household shall be burnt with fire. Therefore, the following morning, as the tribes arrayed themselves, Yahweh showed me it was of the tribe of Judah, the clan of the Zarhites, the household of Zabdi, and the man Achan. Achan confessed to me that he had sinned against Yahweh and stolen a fine Babylonian garment, silver, and gold, and buried them under the floor of his tent. I then sent messengers, who

confirmed that the goods were there, as Achan had said. So those things, Achan, his sons and daughters, his animals, and all of his stuff were taken to the valley of Achor where all of Israel stoned them, burnt them with fire, and raised a heap of stones over them. Thus, Yahweh's anger was turned away. (Joshua 7:13-26)

"This all happened because Achan violated the covenant and God-given commands regarding the first conquest in Canaan. Also, I must admit that I and the messengers that I sent to Ai used our own reasoning regarding how to take Ai. I thought of how we had taken Jericho and presumed we could easily take Ai, a much smaller city. In the process, I did not confer with Yahweh. I also did not call on the high priest to don the ephod and inquire of the Urim and Thummim stones attached to the ephod. If I had done that first, I would have known that Yahweh was angry with us because of the transgression of Achan in stealing for himself both that which was cursed and the silver and gold that was to be devoted to Yahweh and to be put in the treasury of the Tabernacle, because Jericho was the first conquest in Canaan and the first things belong to Yahweh. In that way, neither would lives have been lost, and there would have been no defeat at Ai, nor would the other kingdoms in Canaan stop fearing Yahweh and resolve to attack us.

"But Yahweh is merciful. After the matter of Achan was dealt with, Yahweh spoke to me,

Joshua, and assured me that He had given Ai, its king, and people into our hands. Once again, Yahweh told me not to be fearful or dismayed. Neither should our warriors be afraid or downcast. Also, this time, we would be permitted to take the plunder of Ai for ourselves. Following the strategy given by Yahweh, I set an ambush for Ai. I had 30 thousand warriors go behind Ai by night and wait out of sight. Meanwhile, another 5 thousand warriors of Israel lay in wait in a valley west of Ai. In the morning, I took another force to the gates of Ai. When the men of Ai came out against us, we acted as if we were fleeing before them, as happened previously. As they chased us, the 30 thousand came out of hiding, at my signal, and went into the undefended city. Once the men of Ai ran after us and left Ai open and undefended, I turned and stretched out the spear in my hand toward Ai, as Yahweh had instructed me to do. I kept my spear stretched toward Ai until all 12 thousand inhabitants were slain, both men and women. Those who had chased us turned to see the smoke going up from their city. They had no place to go and were trapped between our three forces, which killed them all. Only the cattle and plunder were taken. The king of Ai was captured and brought to me. There, I had him hung from a tree until the evening when he was cut down and covered with a pile of stones as a memorial. (Joshua 8:1-29)

"Perhaps, because of our initial defeat by the tiny kingdom of Ai and the fact that the

presence of Yahweh was no longer seen over the Tabernacle in our camp as a cloudy pillar by day and a pillar of fire by night, the other kingdoms of Canaan conspired to come together and attack us. Thus, the Hittites, Amorites, Canaanites, Perizzites, Hivites, and the Jebusites formed a military alliance aimed at destroying the people of Israel before we could defeat them in order, one after the other. (Joshua 9:1-2)

"The people of Gibeon were both Hivites and Amorites and lived in four cities, of which Gibeon was the capital. When they heard what we had done to Jericho and Ai after defeating those kingdoms on the east side of the Jordan River, they came to me at our camp in Gilgal, using their wiles, saying they had come as ambassadors from a far country, after a long journey to ally themselves with us. As proof, they had us look at their worn garments and shoes from their journey and the bread they brought to share with us that had become old and moldy. They feigned to be in awe of Yahweh after hearing what He had done for us in bringing us out of Egypt and exterminating the Amorite kingdoms east of the Jordan River. Therefore, I and the leaders of the tribes of Israel made peace with them and entered into a league with their people. We did this on the strength of our own reasoning and did not seek the counsel of Yahweh or have the high priest consult the Urim and Thummim stones on the ephod. That was a mistake, especially after the bitter lesson learned at Ai when I and the tribal

leaders presumed we could handle things without taking counsel of Yahweh. (Joshua 9:3-15)

"Three days after we had entered into a league with the Gibeonites, we learned that they were near neighbors as we moved on to possess the land. The people of Israel were angry with the tribal leaders for entering into a league with the Gibeonites. But the princes of the tribes responded by saying, 'We swore an oath by Yahweh. Who knows what terrible thing will come on us if we break the oath?' The tribal leaders proposed a compromise that would allow the Gibeonites to live, but they would have to become slaves, hewing wood and drawing water for all of

Israel. (Joshua 9:16-21)

"I then summoned the leaders of the Gibeonites and rebuked them for their trickery. I placed a curse on them that they would be as bond slaves without the opportunity to ever have freedom, and it would be their lot to hew wood and draw water for the Tabernacle at Gilgal and the people.

"The Gibeonite leaders were contrite and confessed that they deceived us for fear of their lives because they knew that Yahweh had commanded Moses to give the land to the people of Israel and destroy all of its inhabitants in the process. In meekness, they submitted to their fate. By assigning them to be hewers of wood and drawers of water for all of Israel, I saved them

from the wrath of the people who wanted to ignore the league we had sworn by Yahweh and kill them all. (Joshua 9:22-27)

CHAPTER 22

God Fights for Israel and Exalts Joshua

A Swift Campaign to Take Canaan

"Five Amorite kings, led by Adonizedek, the king of Jerusalem, and including the kings of Hebron, Jarmuth, Lachish, and Eglon, came together to attack Gibeon because of the peace treaty it made with me. They heard what we had done to Jericho and Ai and decided to make war with the cities of Gibeon as a warning to other kings not to make peace with Israel. When they arrived with their armies and surrounded Gibeon, the men of Gibeon sent messengers to me at our camp in Gilgal saying to me,' Come quickly and save us because all of the Amorite kings from the mountains are arrayed against us to make war.' In response, I went up from Gilgal to Gibeon with our whole army and our best warriors. (Joshua 10:1-7)

"Yahweh spoke to me, Joshua, saying, 'Do not be afraid. I have delivered the Amorite armies into your hand. No one will be able to stand up to you on the battlefield.' Therefore, I had the full army of Israel march all night. When we set upon the Amorite armies at Gibeon, we slaughtered them and chased them back toward where they came from. Yahweh also fought for us that day by

throwing down large hailstones upon the Amorite armies such that more of the enemy died from the hailstones than we had killed by our own hands with our swords. Still, the Amorites fled before us as we chased them and cut them down. The day of battle had been long, and I didn't want any Amorite warriors to escape because darkness was approaching. After speaking with Yahweh, I stretched out my spear toward the sun and said out loud where the army of Israel could hear me saying, 'Sun, you stand still over Gibeon and Moon; you stand still in the Valley of Ajalon.' The sun and moon obeyed my words and held in place for about an entire extra day until the army of Israel finished off the Amorite armies. There had never been a day like that before where Yahweh listened to a man and fought for Israel. (Joshua 10:8-14)

"As we fought against the Amorite armies, word came to me that the five Amorite kings had hidden in a cave at Makkedah. I ordered our men to roll huge stones over the mouth of the cave and leave a guard there while the rest of our army pursued the Amorites. We carried out a great slaughter, but some remnants of the Amorite armies made their way into fenced cities. When we returned to Makkedah, I ordered the five Amorite kings brought out of the cave there and had the officers of our army each put their feet on the necks of those kings. Afterward, I personally killed those kings. I also charged the army of Israel not to be afraid or downcast but to be strong and courageous because I told them Yahweh would fight against all of the enemies

that they go into battle against. (Joshua 10:15-25)

"That same day that we finished off the five Amorite kings from the mountains, we took the city of Makkedah and its king. Not one soul was left alive in Makkedah, and we did so with the king of Makkedah just as we had done to the king of Jericho. From Makkedah, the whole army of Israel and I went to the city of Libnah and took it. Not one soul was left alive, and we did to its king just as we had done to the king of Jericho. From Libnah, we marched on to Lachish and did what we had done in Libnah with them on the second day. Horam, the king of Gezer, came with the idea of helping the king of Lachish, but I annihilated him and his people with him.

"From Lachish, the whole camp of Israel went with me to Eglon. We camped there and then killed everyone in it, just as we had done in Lachish. From Eglon, the whole camp of Israel went with me to Hebron. There, we exterminated everyone in Hebron, including its king and all those in the surrounding smaller towns. Then, the whole camp of Israel and I went with me to Debir. We took its king and did with him and the inhabitants as we had done with Hebron and Libnah. Thus, in this one military campaign of conquest, I took all of the hill country, the south, the valley, the springs of water, and those kings. Nothing that breathed was left alive as Yahweh had commanded. Afterward, the whole camp of Israel and I returned to Gilgal. (Joshua 10:25-43)

"Jabin, the king of Hazor, was a great king over many kings. When he heard what I and Israel had done to the Amorite kings of the mountains he sent for Jobab, the king of Madon, and for the king of Shimron, and for the king of Achshaph, he also sent for the kings north of the mountains, from the plains south of Chinneroth, and in the valley and to the border of Dor in the west. He sent for the Amorites, the Hittites, Perizzites, and Jebusites in the mountains and to the Hivites at the base of Hermon in the land of Mizpeh. They came as a great multitude with horses and chariots and many warriors. They pitched their tents at the waters of Merom in preparation for battle with Israel. But Yahweh spoke to me, Joshua, saying, 'Do not be afraid of them because by this time tomorrow, I will cause them to be slain before Israel. Then you will hobble their horses and burn their chariots.' (Joshua 11:1-6)

"After I received Yahweh's words, I took the whole army of Israel to the waters of Merom, where we quickly attacked that large, allied army that had come against us. We cut them down and chased them all the way to Zidon in the north, to Misrephothmaim, and to the valley of Mizpeh eastward. We did not leave any alive. After doing to their horses and chariots as Yahweh had instructed, we returned to Hazor and put its king and people to the sword. Then we burned Hazor down. Hazor was the only city that we burned. All of the other cities we kept along with their cattle. I left nothing undone of what Yahweh had commanded Moses, which Moses then commanded me to do. All of that conquered land

we took: the hill country, the south country, the valley, the plains, and the mountains and valleys up to the border with Lebanon under Mount Hermon. Other than with the people of Gibeon, there was not one people that I made peace with. Instead, we took them in battle. (Joshua 11:7-20)

"As for the Anakim, a race of giants, we proceeded to wipe them out from the mountains, from Hebron, from Debir, from Anab, and all the mountains of Israel. We annihilated them, along with their cities. Thus, Anakim were left only in Gaza, Gath, and Ashdod along the coast of the Great Sea and to the south. After that season of warfare, we rested from the war." (Joshua 11:21-23)

CHAPTER 23

Dividing the Land by Inheritance

"After years of rest from warfare, Yahweh spoke to me, Joshua, saying, 'You are old now and up in years. There still remains a lot of land to be possessed.' After describing in detail the lands yet to be taken, Yahweh said to me, 'I will drive the other inhabitants of the land out before the people of Israel but divide the land by lot as an inheritance as I had commanded you to do.' (Joshua 13:1-6)

"The land was to be divided among the nine and one-half tribes because Moses had given the tribes of Reuben, Gad, and the half-tribe of Manasseh the land they requested east of the Jordan River as their inheritance. The tribe of Levi was not given land like the others because Yahweh's burnt offering sacrifices was their inheritance. The kingdom that had been conquered from King Og in Bashan, east of the Jordan River had a remnant of the giants, but they were exterminated under Moses. Nevertheless, the Geshurites and Maachathites of that land were not expelled and lived among the people of Israel. The lands of the conquered king of Sihon on the east side of the Jordan River, together with the land of Midian, which schemed with Balaam against the people of Israel, were given to the tribe of Reuben. (Joshua 13:7-33)

"The nine and one-half tribes in Canaan west of the Jordan River had the land divided among them by lot for their inheritance as Yahweh had commanded. Before that time, when he was 85 years old, and I was 80 years old, my old friend Caleb of the tribe of Judah requested the land around Hebron as an inheritance. That land had Anakim giants there, and Hebron was formerly named Kirjatharba after a great man named Arba, who was among the Anakim giants there. Caleb said he was as strong as he was when he was 45 years old, and Moses sent him with me and 10 other spies to go through Canaan and report back. Caleb went to a mountainous area where giants lived, but he killed them all, and that land had peace from warfare. (Joshua 14:1-15; and 15:13-15)

"The inheritance lot for the tribe of Judah was large and went all the way to the Great Sea and down to the river bordering Egypt. It included many cities, including the principal cities of the Philistines. But the Jebusites in Jerusalem were not driven out of their fortified stronghold. Since the tribe of Judah could not drive out the Jebusites, the Jebusites were left at Jerusalem with the people of Judah. (Joshua 15:20-63)

"The tribe of Ephraim, of which I was a part, being many, also was assigned a large area with many cities. Since I was unmarried and had no children, as did my friend Caleb, I claimed no large swath of land for my inheritance. Nevertheless, the men of Ephraim could not drive out the Canaanites that lived in Gezer. Instead,

they allowed them to live among them but had to pay tribute. (Joshua 16:1-10)

"When assigning inheritances by lot to the tribe of Manasseh, the daughters of Zelophehad, came to me and Eleazar, the high priest, and reminded us, before the princes of the tribes, that Moses sought Yahweh on their behalf and was commanded of Yahweh to give them an inheritance because their father had no sons. We honored Yahweh's commandment and gave them an inheritance equal to what was given to the men of Manasseh. (Joshua 17:3-6)

"Regretfully, the men of Manasseh could not drive out the Canaanites from certain cities. Instead, they eventually allowed them to live there if they paid tribute but did not completely drive them out. (Joshua 17:12-13)

"Because Ephraim and Manasseh, the two tribes of Joseph, were a large group, they were given two lots. Even so, the men of Ephraim, my own tribe, complained that they were a great people and needed more. I responded by saying, 'If you are so great of a people, then take also the land of the Perizzites and giants.' Still, they complained that the Canaanites living in the valleys assigned to them had iron chariots. Nevertheless, I charged them to drive out the Canaanite Perizzites, even though they had iron chariots and were a strong people. (Joshua 17:14-18)

The Tabernacle and Ark Relocated from Gilgal to Shiloh

"We subsequently moved the whole camp from Gilgal to Shiloh, within the borders of the land allotted to the tribe of Ephraim, my home tribe. The Tabernacle and the Ark of the Covenant thus moved permanently from Gilgal, where we entered after crossing the Jordan River, to Shiloh, which was more centrally located. The Canaanites had been driven from the area around Shiloh. However, we still needed to give seven remaining tribes their inheritance in the land. I upbraided the men of Israel, saying, 'How long will you hesitate in going to possess the rest of the land that the God of your ancestors has given you?' I then had those seven tribes, not including the Levites, select three men from each tribe to go and survey the remaining land, dividing it into seven parcels, and report back to me. When they finished their survey, they returned to me and the rest of the people at Shiloh and presented a book in which they recorded their work, including all of the cities in the seven parcels of remaining land not yet possessed. I then cast lots to divide those seven parcels among the seven tribes that did not yet have an inheritance. (Joshua 18:1-10)

"When the land was assigned by lot, the people decided to give me, Joshua, an inheritance in the city of Timnathserah in Mount Ephraim. So, I built a city there and an estate to live in for myself. (Joshua 19:49-50)

"Yahweh then spoke to me to appoint 12 cities of refuge as Yahweh had told Moses to do. The purpose of these cities was so that if an Israelite or foreigner unwittingly committed manslaughter, he could flee to such a city and be safe from those who would avenge the blood of the one who was killed unwittingly. (Joshua 20:1-9)

"Finally, the tribal leaders of Levi came to me, Joshua, and Eleazar, the high priest at Shiloh. They reminded us that Yahweh had told Moses that the Levites were to be given cities and the suburbs of those cities to dwell in, raise food, and have cattle in the suburbs. Each tribe then assigned cities to the Levites of the clans of Kohath, Gershon, and Merari; 48 cities in all with their suburbs." (Joshua 21:1-45)

CHAPTER 24

Civil War Averted

"After the land was divided by lot, I, Joshua, summoned the tribes of Reuben, Gad, and the half-tribe of Manasseh, which had chosen to take the conquered lands east of the Jordan River as their inheritance. I told them, saying, 'You have kept your vow to Moses and have obeyed all that I have commanded you to do. Now that Yahweh has given rest to your brothers on this side of the Jordan, I release you to return to your tents and to the land you have chosen to possess on the other side of the Jordan River. But be sure to keep the Law of Moses and love Yahweh, your God. Walk in His ways, hold close to Him, and serve Him with your whole heart and all of your soul.' Then, I blessed them and sent them away. (Joshua 22:1-6)

"When the men of Reuben, Gad, and the half tribe of Manasseh returned to the land on the east side of the Jordan River, they erected an enormous altar by the Jordan River. This disturbed the tribes in Canaan, west of the Jordan River. The Tabernacle of Moses and the Ark of the Covenant, along with the brass altar, were now at Shiloh, having been moved years ago from Gilgal when the people of Israel first crossed over into Canaan by way of Yahweh's mighty miracle of making a way through the Jordan River, which was at floodtide at the time. The tribes in Canaan gathered at Shiloh and declared

they were prepared to go to war with the tribes of Reuben, Gad, and the half-tribe of Manasseh for the reason of this breach. It seemed that those on the other side of Jordan wanted to establish an alternative to the place of worship at Shiloh. Each of the ten tribes in Canaan then sent a chief prince, together with Phinehas, the son of Eleazar, the high priest, to confront those on the other side of the Jordan River. Those princes strongly rebuked their brothers on the other side of the Jordan River, warning them not to commit a trespass that would bring down Yahweh's judgment on all the people of Israel.

"The princes of Reuben, Gad, and the half tribe of Manasseh responded by saying they had no intention to rebel against Yahweh or to make sacrifices at their altar. Rather, the altar is a memorial that the Jordan River would not become a cause of division between our future generations. Phinehas and the princes from east of the Jordan River were pleased with what they heard and were satisfied that the wrath of Yahweh would not fall on all of the people of Israel. Thus, Phinehas and the princes departed in peace from Gilead, after which the land west of the Jordan River was called, and returned to Canaan with the news that a civil war was not required. For their part, the people of the tribes of Reuben, Gad, and the half tribe of Manasseh called the altar they had raised up Ed, as a witness between all of the tribes of Israel that Yahweh is God."

CHAPTER 25

Joshua's Farewell Address and Prophesy

"As the end of my life drew near, I, Joshua, summoned all Israel to Shechem, together with their elders, heads, judges, and officers. I chose Shechem because it was where Abraham stopped when he entered Canaan. There, Yahweh appeared to him and made a covenant with him, promising to give the land to his descendants. Also, when Jacob returned from exile with his wives and sons, he made an altar there, naming it El Elohe Israel, which means 'God, the God of Israel.' (Genesis 33:20) Shechem was also where we buried Joseph's bones after we departed Egypt and settled in the promised land of Canaan.

Panoramic view of Shechem ID 127509404 (c) Rumata7 Dreamstime.com

"Once gathered there, I said, 'This is what the Lord God of Israel says to you.' I then proceeded to recount, in the words of Yahweh,

how He chose Abraham, after Noah's flood, from a people that served other gods, led him to Canaan, and multiplied his offspring. Yahweh gave us the patriarchs. As He did with Abraham, Yahweh promised the land of Canaan to Isaac and Jacob and their descendants. After Jacob and his children went to Egypt for over 400 years, He sent Moses and Aaron to bring these people out of Egypt. With mighty wonders, Yahweh brought your fathers out of Egypt, and when the Egyptian army of Pharoah with its chariots and calvary chased you down to the Red Sea, Yahweh put darkness between them and you and then had the sea close upon them when they assayed to capture you and return you to heavy bondage. Of these latter things, I, Joshua, was an eyewitness. You dwelt in the desert wilderness for many years. Yahweh brought you into the land of the Amorites west of the Jordan River. When the Amorites fought with you, Yahweh destroyed them before you. Likewise, when the king of Moab warred against you and called on Balaam to curse you, Yahweh caused Balaam to bless you instead. When you crossed the Jordan River and came to Jericho, where the men of Jericho fought against you, Yahweh delivered them together with the Amorites, the Perizzites, the Canaanites, the Hittites, the Girgashites, the Hivites, and the Jebusites into your hands. Moreover, Yahweh sent swarms of hornets ahead of you to drive them out before you.

The People Warned to Serve God or Be Cursed

"Yahweh has given you a land you did not have to work for, cities you did not build, and vineyards and olive groves to eat from that you did not plant. Therefore, serve Yahweh without pretense or deceitfulness. Put away from you the gods that your ancestors served before Noah's flood and while you were in Egypt. Serve Yahweh! Now then, if you don't think it is a good bargain to serve Yahweh, decide now who you will serve—the gods your ancestors served before Noah's flood or the gods of Egypt—or serve Yahweh. If you think there is no benefit in serving Yahweh, decide now whether you will serve the gods your ancestors served before Noah's flood or the gods of the Amorites in whose land you now dwell. But as for me and my kin, we will serve Adonai, the LORD, Yahweh, the God of Israel.

"The people gathered at Shechem answered in unison, 'God forbid that we should turn our backs on Adonai and submit ourselves to other gods. It is Yahweh, our God, who brought us and our fathers up out of the bondage of Egypt with miraculous signs and wonders that we saw with our own eyes. He is the one who preserved us wherever we went and drove out the people who dwelt in the land, even the Amorites. Therefore, we too will serve the LORD our God.'

"I warned them that He is holy and He is a jealous God. I pronounced a curse on them should they turn their backs on Yahweh to serve strange gods. However, they swore, 'Not so! We will serve the LORD.'

"Again, I charged them to put away the strange gods in their possession, and they swore again to keep the covenant we affirmed that day. Before they departed back to their homes, I set up a memorial stone as a witness to the covenant we made that day."

What's Next?

After Joshua had finished relating the story of God's people and his own story in that saga, the children said, "What's next?"

"What's next? Replied Joshua. "Why you are next. You and those of your generation must live and write the continuing chronicle of our nation.

"How do we do that?" asked Ephraim.

"The same way I did," said Joshua. "By seeking God's face and His guidance every step of the way. Keep the precepts and ordinances of God that Yahweh handed down through Moses, and never stray from Him to worship the gods of the Canaanites, the gods of the Egyptians, or the gods of any other nation that Yahweh delivered you from in order to bring you to this place. And finally, As Yahweh told me, 'Be strong and of good courage.'"

Epilogue

This book chronicles the life journey of Joshua, the son of Nun, of the tribe of Ephraim, a branch of Joseph. We have followed Joshua from slave pits to the heights of direct communication with God. Moses selected Joshua to lead the people in battle and accompany him on the most intimate interactions with God. It was a preparation because, in the end, God chose Joshua to carry on even before the imminent death of Moses. God promised Joshua He would be with him as He was with Moses, then did great miracles and wonders to back up that promise. This began with the first entrance into the promised land, holding up the flood waters of the Jordan River to cross over with three million souls on dry land. Then, the greatest was to pause the solar system for an extra day so that Joshua's army could utterly defeat his adversaries in the light of day. This caused the people to fall in line and pledge obedience to the leading of Joshua. Joshua's obituary could have read, "He was faithful and did all that God commanded him to do."

Joshua witnessed the difficulties Moses encountered leading a stubborn and disobedient people who constantly complained against God and His servant Moses. For that reason, the generation before him, his cohort, and the generation coming up behind Joshua all perished in the desert over the span of 40 years. Some died suddenly as God's wrath incinerated them

instantly, opened the earth to swallow them up and then close up over them, sent plagues among them, or just allowed them to die naturally in the course of the journey. In the end, Joshua stood alone at the head of a young nation as the father of the nation and the intermediary with God.

Joshua ensured that they observed all of the laws, statutes, and annual feasts God gave Moses to present to the people. Still, blood sacrifices and offerings were a regular feature of life. This was because the people who came out of Egypt with Joshua were as pagan as the Egyptians. Their children were no exception, requiring Joshua to command them, as he neared the end of his life's journey, to put away the false gods they still carried with them. (Amos 5:25-27)

Some have derisively called the system that God set up with Moses a slaughterhouse religion. The blood of animal sacrifices was continual, even on a good day. The peoples' sins were many and kept them from approaching a holy God. Those animal sacrifices could never take away sin, but they looked forward to the once and for all sacrifice of the life and blood of Jesus Christ. His name in Hebrew, Yeshua, was the same as Joshua's, and both mean Yahweh is salvation. John the Baptist testified that Jesus was the Messiah or Christ by saying, "Look, there is the lamb of God!" (John 1: 36) The writer of Hebrews declared that Jesus, the Messiah, offered himself up once to bear the sins of many and in so doing established a new covenant. (Hebrews 9: 22-28 and Isaiah 53:1-12)

As Moses spoke with God as one speaks face to face with a friend, Jesus had communion with Father God of the triune godhead, except for the moment that the sins of the world were poured out on Jesus on a cross of crucifixion. The Father caused him to suffer the punishment for our sins so that Jesus would become our righteousness that would allow us to enter intimate fellowship with the godhead, if we turn from our sins and accept the saving work of Jesus. Joshua witnessed Moses often intercede for the people so that God would not destroy them. Jesus forever lives to make intercession for us. (Hebrews 7:25) He fulfilled all prophecies concerning him and was obedient to the point of death to save us. He is our salvation and our righteousness. Joshua and the Hebrew people were taken out of Egypt. Similarly, the prophet Hosea, speaking God's words, said, "I called my son out of Egypt." (Hosea 11:1 and Matthew 2:15) Joshua foreshadowed Jesus as the one who took us to a promised better place and established the peace of God.

About the Author

Louis McCall was born in Chicago, Illinois, and attended Northwestern University, where he received a Ph.D. in political science. Later, he also attended the National War College of the National Defense University. Louis was an Assistant Professor at the Ohio State University in the Department of Political Science prior to a thirty-six-year career in the U.S. Department of State, first as a Foreign Service officer and then as a foreign affairs Civil Service employee where he served as Consul General in Florence, Italy, Charge d'Affaires in Brunei, U.S. Representative to the Republic of San Marino, and Assistant Inspector General. He lived in or worked in, at least temporarily, more than sixty countries on six continents. Whether in academia or as a diplomat, Louis found opportunities to live his faith, including parttime ministry of the good news in word and in song, including co-laboring with missionaries, national church leaders, and the underground church. When ministering early in his diplomatic career from the pulpit of a great church in Calcutta, India, Louis said to those in attendance that he had determined not to be ashamed of the gospel of Christ. That has been a commitment he has endeavored to keep over the years. In his final two years at the Department of State, he organized and led the National Day of Prayer observances in the Department.

Now, in his new career as an author, he has the pleasure of greater freedom in sharing what God has placed in his heart. Louis is active simultaneously in two churches in Washington, D.C. One is a multi-site non-denominational church, and the other is a Catholic church where he is a regular cantor, though not a Catholic himself. He has managed this with the blessing and full knowledge of pastors and priests. This has been an outgrowth of his early association with a mixed protestant-Catholic charismatic house-based worship group, his association with the late Saint Mother Teresa of Calcutta, his charismatic Catholic wife, Lenora, and guest ministry in churches and bible schools of various denominations while living in or working in other countries.

Louis is the author of According to Your Word Lord, I Pray; The Epic of God; He Chose the Glory: The Life and Legacy of Obed-Edom; World Upside Down: The Life of Paul, God's Chosen Messenger, and Mary: Intimate Witness to God's Love Incarnate.

I truly hope you enjoyed this book. It was written for you. Please recommend it to others. I also welcome your feedback. It would really encourage me to hear from you. You can follow me on my website and on social media using the links below.

Website: www.louiismccallinternational.com
Address: Louis McCall International, P.O. Box 60211, Washington, DC 20039 X: @DrLouisMcCall

End Notes

[1]   We Were Slaves to the Hyksos in Egypt, by Joseph Weinstein, The Torah.com; 9 Facts About the Enigmatic Hyksos Invaders of Ancient Egypt, Greg Beyer, The Collector, April 18, 2023.

[2]   Hatshepsut, Bible and Spade, Winter 2003; and Some Images of the King and Queen Together in Stele of Ahmose I, Bill Manley, Trabajos de Egiptologia, Papers on Ancient Egypt, Numero 1, 2002. [3] Who Was the Pharaoh of the Exodus?, Christopher Earmes, Let the Stones Speak, March-April 2023.

[4]   Who Was the Pharaoh of the Exodus?, Christopher Earmes, Let the Stones Speak, March-April 2023.

[5]   Who Was the Pharaoh of the Exodus?, Christopher Earmes, Let the Stones Speak, March-April 2023.

www.ingramcontent.com/pod-product-compliance
Lightning Source LLC
Chambersburg PA
CBHW041158150726
48006CB00016B/2031